HOW TO
MAKE
THE
RIGHT
DECISIONS

HOW TO
MAKE
THE
RIGHT
DECISIONS

John D. Arnold   Bert L. Tompkins

MOTT MEDIA

HOW TO MAKE THE RIGHT DECISIONS

Leonard George Goss, Editor

Designed by Kurt Dietsch
Manuscript editing by Leonard G. Goss and Leslie H. Stobbe
Typesetting by Joyce Bohn

Manufactured in the United States of America

ISBN 0-915134-82-9

TABLE OF CONTENTS

PREFACE

"The heart of the wise teacheth his mouth, and addeth learning to his lips."

(Proverbs 16:23)

"Good" decisions are perceived by many people as being made only in the cold light of "logic" carefully exercised by the rational mind and insulated from the personal feelings and values of the decision maker. As we are admonished by some hard-fisted business executives and decision making "experts," "Don't let your heart rule your head!" It's as though there is no place in the decision-making process for expressing spiritual values, love of God and fellow man, and personal moral convictions.

One of *our* personal convictions is that the decisions of greatest wisdom are those which represent an integration of the "heart" *and* the "mind," the necessary two lenses with which all of us view the world if we wish to do so in balance.

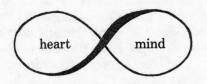

Accordingly, we have developed a decision process which helps those faced with making an important decision and bringing into proper balance spiritual, logical, and emotional influences to choose the *best* course of action.

This balanced, integrative feature (heart ∞ mind) of our decision-making and communication process was first published in John's book, *"Make Up Your Mind"* (Amacom, 1978), which caught the attention and interest of Mr. George Mott, our publisher, who immediately made use of several of the decision tools and found them practical and helpful. He prevailed upon us to write a book that would focus particularly on helping Christian men and women throughout the world make decisions they could really feel confident about, assured in their hearts they made the "right" choice *before* taking action.

John D. Arnold is founder and President of John Arnold ExecuTrak Systems, Inc., Waltham, Mass., a decision-making/planning/problem-solving/communications firm of counselors to senior management which also conducts many training programs. For more than a decade, he has served as personal counselor to presidents and other top executives of many multinational corporations and smaller entrepreneurial companies as well as for not-for-profit organizations and government agencies. John developed the decision-making process that is the focus of this book. Many clients have discovered with his help that the decision-making principles, questions, and techniques are as applicable to making everyday personal and family decisions as they are to making complex, many-faceted business, civic, and governmental decisions.

Elbert Tompkins, Senior Associate and Director of Research and Development of John Arnold ExecuTrak Systems, joined the firm in 1968 shortly after its inception and has been involved in all phases of executive counseling and development. Bert's business career has required several relocations with his family and has provided him the opportunity to serve on numerous church committees as both committee member and chairman, and as a trustee in several different churches where he has been able to make significant applications of the decision tools and concepts you will be reading about.

Among the qualifications we have for writing this book are our experiences—and those of countless others over the years who have shared with us their disappointments and frustrations—working with well-intentioned members of church groups who failed to benefit from one another's talents, skills, and know-how; who have wasted valuable time, become divisive, and who were generally ineffective in carrying out their church responsibilities. We have also worked with individuals who unwittingly hurt others, damaged personal relationships, and compromised their principles through some of their decisions—and who suffered great remorse *after* the fact.

Our sincere hope is that this book will help people in all walks of life avoid such regrettable consequences in their individual and collaborative decision-making.

How to Make the Right Decisions is divided into three sections:

Section I (Chapters 1 and 2) reminds us that God has given us able minds to determine and evaluate options, along with understanding the ultimate responsibility for our decisions. This section explains the many difficulties prople have in making decisions and further explains why a systematic decision-making method is necessary. It also includes numerous suggestions to help readers take stock of their strengths and weaknesses, to more clearly and consistently bring the meaning and purpose of their lives into the decisions they make everyday, as well as those crucial "once-in-a-lifetime" decisions.

Section II (Chapters 3 through 9) explains in detail our seven-step decision-making process. It has been tested and proven of value to thousands of people as they struggled with important decisions of spiritual, moral, personal, or financial consequence. The section describes how men and women have applied these decision-making techniques individually and in groups to "thinking through" the issues and opportunities facing them, confidently reaching decisions reflecting their personal values.

Section III (Chapters 10 through 13) focuses primarily upon how you can help others make decisions. It addresses such questions as: "When is involving others in decision-making most helpful?"; "When should I *avoid* involving others?"; "How can I make the *best* use of other help in decision-making?"; "What should I do when I have to make a *quick* decision?"; and "How can I apply the decision-making process in helping another make a decision?"

The "personalities" you will meet in this book include:

a. Doug and Sherry: when Doug was offered a job promotion in another part of the country, they were faced with deciding what to do about an opportunity that would provide increased income and professional growth but could seriously disrupt their family life, the lives of their children, their friendships, and their ties to their church and community.

b. The young president of a company whose systematic rethinking of a key business decision may well have saved his business, his marriage, and the love of his children.

c. The father who made an all-too-costly decision that he actually didn't have to make.

d. The President of the Board of Directors of a social agency who had to decide whether a valued member of the staff should be discharged because of a serious breach of agency policy, thereby jeopardizing an important community service offered by the agency.

e. Dick and Barbara: they had to make extremely difficult decisions for themselves and their young family following the medical diagnosis of Barbara's terminal cancer.

f. The President of a large corporation who accepted a decision by the Board of Directors as perhaps appropriate for that company but which violated his Christian convictions, and so resigned his presidency.

g. The pastor who—by skillful, patient, and systematic guidance of a Youth Director Selection Committee—achieved unamimous agreement on a decision that could have been riddled with conflicts and unhappiness.

For the important role they have played in the preparation and editing of this book, we are indebted to Len Goss and Les Stobbe. To our publisher George Mott, President of Mott

Media, we are also indebted for his encouragement to write this book and his faith in its value to his readers. We are grateful also to Anne Mooradian and Sandra Shulman for their diligence and excellence in the typing of manuscript and for their many constructive comments. And finally, we feel blessed by a working relationship with one another since 1968 which has been marked by continual mutual respect and patient, good-humored exchange of ideas and criticism.

John D. Arnold   Bert Tompkins
January 11, 1982, Waltham, Mass.

Section I

OUR DECISION-MAKING RESPONSIBILITY

Chapter 1

WHAT'S IN A DECISION?

Doug and Sherry were having a last cup of coffee after supper. With the children busy at various assignments, they could get in some of that communication marriage counselors always talked about.

Taking his cup in both hands, Doug fidgeted with the handle as he tried to find the best words for the news he had to spring on his unsuspecting wife. Finally he looked up at her and said quietly, "I've been offered a promotion."

"Honey, that's marvelous! I'm so glad for you. But you don't look very happy about it," Sherry said, her eyes searching her husband's face. He had an obvious worried look about him.

"It means moving to New Hampshire," Doug said, without a trace of excitement in his voice. "They might as well have asked us to move to Australia."

"Well," Sherry said brightly, clearly determined to show her support for her husband, "After California our kids will certainly have a lot of new experiences."

Doug appreciated Sherry's attempt to put the best face on the situation, but he had already carried the decision about for two days and for him it meant trouble. Lots of trouble.

"Can you imagine what that would do to us as a family?" Doug asked. "I've just been elected president of the Rotary Club and was really looking forward to implementing some of my ideas. You've finally got the pottery kiln working right and are about to become a famous potter in these parts. Jim made varsity in basketball this year—think he'll want to move? Linda is all excited about her junior high band going to a festival this fall. And Trudy, she's a plodder who is so introspective I'm afraid it would take her years to make new friends."

Doug took a sip of coffee, sloshing the remaining coffee around as though he were trying to read directions from it.

"Well, my Dad always said, 'Let's get the pros and cons down so we can look at them.' He seemed to make pretty good decisions. I'll go get a piece of paper," Sherry said. When Doug was in one of these moods, she knew she would have to take the initiative. In the office Doug seemed to make decisions with ease, but when they involved the family he usually had a tough time.

That evening the two columns on Sherry's paper got rather long. And when the exercise was finished, the decision seemed as far off as when they began.

What was wrong with Sherry's approach? Was it Doug's clearly depressed mood? Had they missed a clear pro or a strongly negative con? What should have gone into their attempt at decision-making? What *is* a decision made up of anyway?

Before we get into the answers to these questions let's see if we can pick up a few pointers from a time for decision described in the Bible. Though it took place nearly three thousand years ago, the incident had all the elements of a classic decision-making situation.

The twelve tribes of Israel had each established their territories in their new land, Canaan, and Joshua was ready to pass on the leadership. He called the elders, judges and officers in the army together. First he told them again how God had led them out of Egypt and into the promised land. He reminded them of God's faithfulness. Then he said, "And if you be unwilling to serve the Lord, choose this day whom you will serve, whether the gods your fathers served in the region beyond the River, or the gods of the Amorites in whose land you dwell; but as for me and my house we will serve the Lord" (Joshua 24:15 RSV). How well, or how badly, the leaders of the people chose can be seen in the next book of the Bible, Judges, even though it would appear from verse 24 that they made the right choice.

The fact that the leaders of Israel had a choice that day, and that Doug and Sherry had a choice, reveals several elements in decision-making. One is that God has given all of us a mind able to determine the options. If we take the time, we can think through the elements in a situation requiring a decision, evaluating the alternatives. The second is that each decision has automatic consequences once we act upon it. Finally, no one else can make these decisions for us and we bear ultimate responsibility for making them, as did the leaders of Israel facing Joshua that day.

I'll go along with that, you say, but my problem is that I have difficulty making the right decision. As one of the authors writes in his book, *Make Up Your Mind:*

> Considering all the practice we get in making decisions, you would expect that we would be good at making them; the more typing you do, the better typist you become. But the number of decisions you make has nothing to do with your skill at making them or the results you obtain. For the most part, decision-making is an ignored art. We take lessons to learn tennis or golf, but we rely on our own devices to make decisions. It is assumed that decision-making comes naturally, like learning to breathe. It does not.

The freedom to make a decision involving options can get really complicated. Israel had three choices. One was the gods they had left behind in Egypt, the second was the gods of the people they had conquered (some choice, considering Israel had defeated those who trusted those gods!), and the third was the Lord God Jehovah, who had performed enough miracles to make Him a virtual shoo-in, it would seem.

That was a simple choice, you are probably thinking, compared to the dilemma Doug and Sherry faced. At stake was not only growth within the company and the increased income that went with it, but also the uprooting of a whole family with their various community and school activities and relationships. There is no way they could predict all the consequences professionally and for the family of a move across the country into a community with lifestyles radically different from the freewheeling California lifestyle. To have to assume responsibility for those consequences could affect Doug so much that he would lose effectiveness on the job.

Yet Joshua reveals that if we have developed a personal relationship with the God who made us it is easy to make the decision out of which flow all others. After he had rehearsed all that Jehovah had done for Israel in its escape from Egypt, preservation through forty years in the desert and conquest of Canaan, Joshua declares emphatically, "But as for me and my house, we will serve the LORD" (v.15). Once that priority has been established, other priorities can be sorted out with the help of the One who promised," Lo, I am with you always, even to the end of the age" (Matthew 28:20 NASB), before departing to be our advocate with the Father. The effective implementation of this presence of Jesus comes in the manner He promised in John 14:26, "But the Helper, the Holy Spirit, whom the Father will send in My name, He will teach you all things, and bring to your remembrance all that I said to you."

How would this affect Doug and Sherry's decision-making? Does putting God and service to Him first provide automatic answers to complex problems? There are some who say that this is their experience. Yet think of Paul, that great missionary apostle. Consider his desire to visit Rome and preach the message of Christ there, as expressed in Romans 1:10. Even though he was convinced it was the will of God that some day he preach in Rome, his decision was to write a letter because he could not get an immediate answer about when he'd get there. While he waited, he kept busy, doing what he could to live out his great overriding priority to serve Greeks, Jews, even the "barbarians" and bring them to the knowledge of Christ (see Romans 1:14-15).

For most of us, the outworking of our daily priorities in the light of our number one priority to serve God demands some kind of decision-making process. Only when we start to chart our main considerations, the alternatives, weigh the strength of the various options, and consider what could go wrong do we achieve some level of confidence in our decisions. If we are open to the internal nudgings of the Holy Spirit this decision-making process is greatly enhanced.

Also true, however, is that establishing our relationship with

God and service to Him as our number one priority does eliminate some alternatives in decision-making. The Bible is quite clear about a surprising number of activities and often predicts the results of undertaking these activities. That's why, for example, some Christians read a chapter of Proverbs every day—these words of Solomon and others in tune with God provide a surprisingly clear frame of reference for much of what we experience.

Doug and Sherry, however, need to do more than read the book of Proverbs in the Bible. That's why they resorted to listing the pros and cons. In this book we propose an approach to decision-making that goes well beyond the exercise Doug and Sue initiated. And we'll consistently put the various steps in the larger framework provided by the Bible. So stick with us while we lay the groundwork and begin building patterns of decision-making that we have found useful both with simple and complex life situations requiring a decision.

Why Is Decision-Making So Tough?

We are not the first generation to find decision-making tough. Doug and Sherry's parents may not have faced quite as complex a situation, but that did not reduce the level of personal confusion in deciding among various options. Earlier we referred to Paul's confusion about his inability to get to Rome when he was clearly convinced of God's call to preach the Gospel there. Some things were "preventing" him from going. A little further into his letter to the Romans Paul indicates the cause for some of our confusion. He writes, "I find then a law, that when I would do good, evil is present with me. For I delight in the law of God after the inward man: But I see another law in my members warring against the law of my mind, and bringing me into captivity to the law of sin which is in my members" (Romans 7:21-23).

As Paul indicates, the confusion arises because of internal conflict. The root problem is our inability to escape the influence of sinful desire, which conflicts with our desire to serve God. Recognizing this prepares us to tackle other complicating factors affecting our ability to make clear-cut decisions, always aware we have the power of God working in and through us.

In our experience, some of the other factors affecting decision-making are indecisiveness, unwillingness to accept responsibility, the complexity of choices, difficulties in choosing between a good and the best course of action, and our fear that we will not be able to defend the "rightness" of our decision to ourselves and to others.

Let's examine indecisiveness a little more closely. Why did Doug wait several days to break the news of his promotion possibility to Sherry? And why did he wait for Sherry to initiate the decision-making process?

Incredible as it may seem, many people are indecisive because they refuse to accept the fact that a decision is necessary. They hope the situation will resolve itself and not need their involvement.

Clem's parents were like that. Their son had been caught in destruction of property in high school, suspended for attacking a teacher, and finally expelled when he verbally attacked the principal with a stream of obscenities. Barred from the school property, Clem brazenly wandered into the halls on opening day in the fall, surrounded himself with some of his friends and attacked a freshman, breaking his nose before custodians could intervene.

When the freshman's parents called the police to see what could be done, they discovered that Clem's file was an inch thick.

"We've tried again and again to involve Clem's parents in decision-making regarding Clem's future. They refuse to admit that there is a problem. No matter what you say, they refuse to act," the sergeant told the freshman's parents.

This incident reveals a second factor involving indecisiveness, unwillingness to accept responsibility. We know that making a decision makes us responsible for the consequences, and we do not want to get that deep into it.

A less easily recognizable reason for indecisiveness is a feeling that more information is needed. We feel that as long as we are gathering information we can justifiably postpone making the decision.

A company had installed a computer to handle a growing volume of business. For a variety of reasons the person writing the program was not given all the information needed, and it soon became apparent that the information produced was inadequate. Rather than "bite the bullet," the company kept accumulating information on areas in which the program provided inadequate data, making "patches" on the program to make do. After three years of such information gathering the management was still repeating, "Some day we're going to have to rewrite the whole program."

If you had asked management why they had not made the decision to redo the program for the computer, their answer would not have been, "We do not have enough information." They would have responded with an answer highlighting another reason for indecisiveness: the problem is so complex we just cannot tackle it now.

This may well have been another factor in Doug's not telling Sherry about the decision he had to make. He did not need to get far into the ramifications of the move to New Hampshire to be overwhelmed with the complexity of the implications for his family. According to Alvin Toffler, the very nature of contemporary society, with its constant social and technological change, has created a problem of "over-choice." He writes, "Never before have masses of men faced a more complex set of choices. The hunt for identity arises not out of the supposed choicelessness of 'mass society,' but precisely from the plenitude and complexity of our choices."

Being overwhelmed by the complexity of choices can lead to a serious dilemma, again illustrated by Doug. Remember how even after admitting that he had been offered a promotion he kept staring at his cup of coffee? He had become emotionally paralyzed by the fear of making the "right" decision for his family and his own future. At such a time it is easy to develop tunnel vision, focusing on only a few of the possible actions, none of which seem genuinely satisfactory. At such a point we may make a quick decision that we will regret for many years.

When Ann was a little girl her dog bit the mailman, who had a bad habit of teasing the dog when delivering the mail. Acting quickly, her father had the dog destroyed.

"Years later my father admitted that he had often regretted that hasty decision. He had not taken the time to consider the circumstances, especially how much the dog meant to me. I discovered that this one decision troubled him the rest of his life," Ann reported.

The kind of world we live in creates another problem affecting decisiveness in decision-making. No matter how carefully we consider all the options and then enthusiastically embark on the "right" course, this world can never truly completely satisfy all our wants. Consider the energy crisis. The abundance of coal would clearly dictate a swing to coal use—except that much of the coal has a high sulfur content that has already produced the "acid rain." But if we opt for oil or natural gas, we know we have limited resources—and solar energy is not nearly applicable in all cases. Should we then use nuclear energy? Not if we remember Three Mile Island vividly.

Decision-making thus means choosing the "best" from among no satisfactory alternative. Once we have experienced the results of decisions like this we may become so wary that we try to put off the inevitable.

Now if our decision requires acceptance by others, like the three teeners in Doug and Sherry's family, then we may also retreat to indecisiveness. We may be able to reach a decision with which we feel comfortable, but we may not feel up to challenging statements like, "It just isn't right," or "The cost is prohibitive." Like politicians, we send up a "trial balloon" and wait for the fall-out in response from our associates. If we are "shot down" we may very well retreat totally .

Is there a way to convince ourselves and others that we have made a good decision?

What Is a "Good" Decision?

Consider Doug and Sherry. Would it be a good decision if accepting the promotion/move would help set him up for the presidency of the company? What if the move also brought Sherry new opportunities to branch out into other art forms beyond pottery? Of course, being in the East would make the Ivy League schools that much more accessible for the children. Yet what if Trudy, the introvert, does not make new friends— and when she does do so in high school they are drug and alchohol abusers? And what if there is no church with a good youth program for Linda and Jim in the new city? Is it also still a good decision if the promotion revealed that Doug had reached the "level of his incompetence" (the Peter Principle)?

There are, however, several ways to judge the quality of a decision before any of the results are in. The following are criteria we have tested—you may want to add some of your own:

1. A "good" decision inspires initial confidence—you feel good about it.

2. You based your decision on an adequate amount of information. You stopped to ask, "Exactly what is needed to know to make this decision—and how do I get the information?" Unless you have done this you may continue to feel uneasy about your decision.

3. The decision was clearly necessary and directed to the "real" issues.

4. It coincides with what you believe the Bible teaches and with your overriding priority to worship God and serve Him.

5. The decision will best achieve the basic purpose for making the decision and accomplish your goals better than alternatives.

6. It is a well-balanced decision (you achieve what you want to achieve without too great a risk to available resources) and it will not create additional problems.

7. You can support it objectively and defend it logically.

8. You are confident it will be implemented by those on whom its success depends.

Yet how can we achieve a level of decision-making expertise that produces results that make us feel good about what will happen? That will make it possible for us to test our decision against the criteria just listed?

Some people would opt for Doug and Sherry's approach, evaluating the pros and cons. Others are so sure of their experience that they will tell you, "I can trust my intuition." Then there's the outwardly confident person who has it down to a real science—gut feeling. After years of consulting with individuals, providing consulting services to companies and governments, we have developed a systematic approach to decision-making that we are convinced works better than any of the above. Tests of our approach in the most complex decision-making situations verify that there is a way to know you have made a "good" decision. We want to share the freedom this produces with you.

In the following chapters we will introduce you to our decision-making process bit by bit. We will "walk through" a variety of life situations where it was applied, or could be applied. You will grow in confidence that you can actually implement this approach in your life, business and church situations. As you open yourself up to the guidance of the Holy Spirit during the decision-making process you will realize anew that God does not want us to be ignorant of His will.

Chapter 2

WHERE DO I FIT IN?

Have you ever gone the route of Doug and Sherry when faced with a decision important to you? Even though you felt you had listed every pro and con you couldn't seem to get a clear-cut sense of direction. Most of us have, even though we know our exercise should not turn out that way.

What went wrong? In most cases there are a number of factors, but a large majority of us simply started too far down the line in the decision-making process.

Let's consider an analogy from industry. You walk into the new car showroom, check out the various models available, test drive several, and select the model you feel will best meet your needs. You settle down to choosing the options and soon discover that no car on the dealer's premises matches your list. You place an order and wait for delivery. One week before the delivery date you finally get down to business on your vacation plans. Halfway through the process you suddenly realize that you are going to be driving through several hot southern states—and you left off the air conditioning on the car to save money.

The next day you call the dealer, hoping against hope that the air-conditioning unit can still be added on the assembly line. The dealer checks it out, and reveals that the car is already enroute by train. The dealer describes your alternatives—none very attractive.

What was the missing element in your decision-making about what car to get and the options to purchase? The purpose for the car. Yes, you did consider the options you thought you would need. Without a clear statement on what the car represented to you, how it fit into your life experiences, your decision-making was, however, incomplete and faulty.

You, who you are, what purpose and meaning you have in life, in the same way are the most important ingredient in your decision-making process. William A. Charland, Jr., puts it this way: "We need to consider how decision-making fits into the larger context of purpose. Decisions have meaning only as they make sense and fit together in the fabric of some ongoing awareness of what we're about." Sometimes this overarching sense of who we are is called our worldview.

Let's join Doug and Sherry again. Suppose on that first piece of paper placed on the table Sherry had put the heading, "What we are here for." Granted, Doug may not have been ready for that "heavy" a question at that point, but he may well have been able to focus more clearly on it during the next days if he knew Sherry was also exploring the possible answers. When they came together again they might have roughed out an outline like:

—to worship God and serve Him
—to be honest and upright citizens
—to help each other achieve our human potential
—to use the gifts God has given us wisely
—to raise children who can think for themselves

Your own list, if you were to make one, could well be longer and more explicit. Whatever is on that list, it could well be a determining factor in all future decisions.

Nehemiah, that famous city-rebuilder during the period of Jewish resettling in Judah after the Babylonian captivity, serves as an admirable role model. You may remember he was the cupbearer to King Artaxerxes of Persia. One day he checked with one of the travelers from Judah and discovered that Jewish exiles who had returned to Jerusalem earlier were dispirited and subject to abuse by those who had taken over in the area. His prayer to God reveals that he recognized and accepted his Jewishness, he accepted that he bore some responsibility for what had happened, and that God was able to effect change through him and his position at the court. That clarified, he confronted the king.

Notice how the goal he set for himself, which grew out of knowing who he was in both the king's and God's sight, infused his statements and actions from then on. Before the king he says, "Send me to Judah, to the city of my fathers' tombs, that I may rebuild it" (Nehemiah 2:5). Back in Jerusalem he took a ride around the broken down walls of the city and quickly made a decision: "Come, let us rebuild the wall of Jerusalem that we no longer be a reproach" (2:17). When their enemies tried to discourage the people, scare them into stopping work on the wall, Nehemiah told the nobles and the people, "Do not be afraid of them; remember the Lord who is great and awesome" (4:14). Finally, when he was faced with social conditions that favored the rich and oppressed the poor, he called a great assembly and reminded them, "The thing which you are doing is not good; should you not walk in the fear of our God because of the reproach of the nations, our enemies?" (5:9).

As a person conscious of who he was, of his spiritual and national heritage, all Nehemiah's decisions were focused on rebuilding Jerusalem and lifting the cloud of disgrace, the reproach. Personal achievement and safety became secondary to his overarching goal, whereas we tend to make them primary goals.

Who Are We Really?

The obituary page carried the tragic story. A local designer in electronics had come up with a new design for a computerized cash register. Forming his own company, he had raised the capital and started manufacturing the new design. He soon discovered that competing against the giants was tough, eventually selling out to one of them. Some years later the national giant closed his division. Again he started his own company, and again he faced bankruptcy. One day he was found hanging in his own home. Rather than face continuing personal failure in business he took his own life.

This businessman is typical of many people today. Who they are is wrapped up in what they do and can achieve in men's eyes. When they fail to achieve the level of success and recognition they consider essential to personal satisfaction, they give up. They do not recognize their business activity as merely one function of the greater purpose of being, of their role as a person created by God for a larger purpose.

One way of saying this is found in Proverbs 11:3, "The integrity of the upright shall guide them." The word "integrity" could be defined as true to self, making the actions of the upright an extension of their true nature. The Apostle Paul put it in New Testament terms when he wrote, "For the love of Christ controls us . . . therefore we are ambassadors for Christ, as though God were entreating through us; we beg you on behalf of Christ, be reconciled to God" (2 Corinthians 5:14,20). Over and over again in his letters, Paul states that his motivation for decision-making grows out of his love-relationship with God and his resulting role as servant of God.

Modern psychologists and behavioral scientists have recently reached similar conclusions. One of them, Erik Erikson, describes a healthy sense of identity as "the ability to experience one's self as something that has continuity and sameness and to act accordingly." What Erikson is saying is that people want to be part of something bigger than they are.

Members of a Sunday school class who successfully completed a ten-mile walkathon to raise funds for a medical doctor and his staff in a Third World country, were asked why they walked the ten miles. Most said simply, "To see if we could do it." Then why not just walk ten miles any old day? In the ensuing discussion it became clear that the major reason was that this effort went for something "much bigger" than themselves. In fact, the significance went far beyond themselves, their family, their town, and even their nation.

This true experience provides insight into why people participate in experiences "much larger than ourselves." The first is the knowledge that we are capable of greater effort and achievement than we normally give ourselves credit for. The larger purpose helps us extend ourselves for others at a level usually not considered possible. This recognition can be a significant factor in decision-making.

Yet such experiences also reveal that we can achieve at higher levels if we forego self-interest. Walking ten miles on a strictly "for me" basis was not a strong enough motivation. Only when it was for the larger public good of people they did not even know did they get up the courage to embark on the walkathon.

If feeling ourselves as part of the larger purposes of God increases our feelings of self-worth and motivates us in decision-making, the opposite side of the coin is that we must also feel ourselves as unique.

Erich Fromm explains in his writings that much unhappiness among people stems from their inability to experience themselves as "I am" instead of merely "the sum total of other people's expectations." When the latter is true, the person becomes James's "double-minded man, unstable in all his ways" (James 1:8). In contrast, the Apostle Paul was so sure of who he was in God's sight that he could say, "I press toward the goal for the prize of the upward call of God in Jesus Christ" (Philippians 3:14).

Much of the impetus for the feminists in the women's movement stems from their feeling that as women they had been forced to submerge their personal identity in the family, in society, and in business. The same is true of the young people who rebelled in the late sixties and early seventies. In fact, churches today are still losing young people because some of them feel they have lost their self-identity in the pressure to conform to the church's purpose and pattern.

Yet the Bible is very clear that God created man in such a way that each one of us is unique. We all have a different set of genes that result in each one of us being a different personality. When we get into the teaching of the Apostle Paul about the church, this is emphasized even more pointedly. After explaining that the Holy Spirit distributes a variety of gifts to members of Christ's body, he lists these gifts and their expression. He sums up this activity in 1 Corinthians 12:11, "But one and the same Spirit works all these things, distributing to each one individually just as He wills."

Okay, you recognize that you are a part of God's great purpose for the world and that he provided you with the genes and the spiritual gifts to be a unique person. But how can you get a handle on some of the specific purposes and gifts? Let's first see how that larger purpose can be expressed, defined more sharply so it can influence decision-making more directly.

How Do We Express Our Purpose?

Earlier we said that Doug and Sherry started their decision-making too far down the track, that they needed to first consider their overarching purpose in life before they considered pros and cons. Suppose that they had done that and listed some of these purposes. To have them genuinely impact on their decision-making process they now would have to take these purposes a step further and state them in terms of values, goals, and objectives.

Values are a source of meaning and satisfaction in our daily lives, they in fact determine the tone of our decision-making. Take a value like honesty. If Doug and Sherry felt deeply that their personal integrity presupposed honesty as a factor in all their decisions, then it could become part of a goal as well: "Be honest in all things." Or suppose they considered generosity an important value. This could be expressed in a goal like, "Live more simply so we can share."

Such goals influence us throughout a lifetime of activity. They help give direction to what we do, even when at times we feel they are not attainable. If Doug and Sherry's goal was to live more simply a move could help them implement it because of the new setting—and it could become a permanent feature of lifestyle. To be sure they achieved their goal of being honest in all things they would have to examine whether the new position, for example, meant dealings with foreign companies that involved bribery.

Stating objectives brings values and goals into more day-by-day activities, because objectives are more specific than values or goals. Objectives are clearly achievable and measurable. Doug, for example, could insist on honesty in all of his division's sales presentations as an achievable objective. Sherry could insist that marred pottery be marketed as such and not merely touched up and sold as perfect. The sense of personal satisfaction that grows out of achieving such objectives brings with it a genuine sense of personal fulfillment.

Three questions can help us integrate our values into our life as goals and objectives:
1. What values are truly important to me?
2. How can I best express these values as goals?
3. How can I best translate these goals into measurable objectives when I am faced with a decision?

If we have grown up in a Christian environment, gone to church regularly, and studied the Bible occasionally we probably have absorbed a number of biblical values. But until they are tested in the crucible of life we do not know whether they have genuinely become a part of us, or whether we have merely given mental assent to them. That's why values clarification has gained popularity. In Sunday school, in Bible studies and in discussion groups there is a growing practice to put on the table a life situation that represents a crisis. People are asked to respond, indicating how they would act. The responses are measured against biblical injunctions.

You can come to a much clearer understanding of what your values, goals, and objectives are by doing a personal exercise like the following. Answer each question honestly.

1. What is your favorite Bible story? What especially attracts you to this story?

2. What is your favorite Bible verse(s)? What do you see as the central message of this verse(s)?

3. Who are your two favorite persons in the New Testament? Why do you like them?

4. Who is your favorite Old Testament person? What sets this person apart in your mind?

5. What do you pray about most? What does this tell you about yourself?

Once you have honestly answered these questions you can analyze what your values, goals, and objectives are by questions like: a) What specific requirements, qualities, promises expressed have special meaning for me? b) Can I translate any of these into goals for my life? c) What would appear to be my specific goals?

Let's consider what might happen if Doug did this exercise

the day after the fruitless effort to reach a decision using a list of pros and cons. In the process he put down Matthew 22:36-40 as his favorite Bible passage: "Teacher, which is the great commandment in the law? And he said to him, 'You shall love the Lord your God with all your heart, and with all your soul, and with all your mind. This is the great and first commandment. And a second is like it, You shall love your neighbor as yourself. On these two commandments depend all the law and the prophets."

As he analyzed the passage, Doug quickly recognized that one goal was quite clearly to "love the Lord your God with all your heart, and with all your soul, and with all your mind." At that point he bowed his head and made a quick acknowledgement: "Lord, I really do want to love you like that. But when I'm worried about the effect of the move on Trudy, or how Jim might react, I too easily forget that you are Number One. Help me to reestablish this goal." With that he wrote down the objective: "Be sure the new community has a fellowship where we can worship God and express our love for Him."

The other obvious goal was "You shall love your neighbor as yourself." As Doug looked at this statement, he suddenly realized that one reason he had initially responded positively to the move was that he and the neighbor were having a running confrontation over the neighbor's dog. It made a mess of his flower beds—and the front lawn. He decided to state as the objective: "Straighten things out with the neighbor in a spirit of love and consideration."

As the Old Testament personality that really appealed to him, Doug had listed Nehemiah. Analyzing it, he concluded that Nehemiah appealed to him because he saw an opportunity to help his people, and with firm resolve and unwavering courage followed through on that resolve. Doug recognized that the move to New Hampshire appealed to him for that reason as well, since it would involve taking a lagging division in the company and getting it on track again. He knew this would take a lot of wisdom and firm determination.

Suddenly Doug realized that he had earlier almost made a decision against the move without recognizing it as a decision. That was one reason all that bit about pros and cons had been such a fruitless exercise. You see, in thinking about all of the ramifications for the family if they were to move to New Hampshire, he had inadvertently ducked out from under the responsibility to make a decision. Rather than face up to the need for a decision squarely, he had used the children's needs and reactions as an "out" not to make a decision.

All of us are adept at shunting responsibility for the way we are, for the failure to make positive moves forward, onto others. Depressed persons, for example, often choose depression (usually unconsciously). Because this person is now "sick," he or she does not need to accept responsibility for actions that really should be taken. This may cover a feeling of inadequacy, or act as a shield against possible unpleasant consequences. In Doug's case, the depression made it possible to postpone the moment of truth when the decision had to be made and announced to the family.

What Resources Do I Bring?

Now that Doug had come to terms with his purpose in life, crystallized what his values, goals and objectives were (at least to some extent), he faced the next step. Would the promotion truly be in keeping with his personal resources, or would it simply help him reach the "level of his incompetence"? What limitations in his training and experience, his personality make-up, could prevent him from being a success in his new position?

You see, Doug, like most of us, had begun to take himself for granted. Things had been going so smoothly at the office, he had been able to make a satisfying contribution, and there his concern ended. He needed to take stock of his inner resources, the skills he had developed technically and in people relationships.

The promotion and move also presented Sherry with a genuine opportunity for personal growth. She had become so preoccupied with her pottery that she had stagnated in other areas. Working with Doug on the values and goals clarification, she would discover that she was ready for a new challenge.

Yet such self-inventorying is not easy. That's why we are including a tool we developed for this purpose. It represents a synthesis, adaptation and expansion of value clarification work by James McHolland and separate work by Richard N. Bolles in life/career planning. This tool will help you to systematically identify and evaluate your personal resources and limitations.

ANALYSIS OF STRENGTHS AND DEFICIENCIES IN PERSONAL ACHIEVEMENTS AND DISAPPOINTMENTS

1. Think of experiences from several areas of life: family relationships, church, work, hobbies, time spent with close friends. Then in each set of diagonal spaces at the top of the worksheets on pages 23 through 30 list the following:

   a. Five significant personal experiences you, and/or others important to you, acknowledge as successful accomplishments.

   b. Five experiences which brought you personal disappointments.

2. In the first five columns for each of the *accomplishments*, check those personal resources or abilities you feel significantly contributed to your success. You may find it helpful to test your conclusions by discussing them with others.

3. In the five columns for each of the *disappointments* noted, check those resources and abilities which could have significantly helped you turn disappointments into success IF you had been stronger in these abilities or more alert to proper resources.

4. Finally, review the chart with these questions in mind:

   a. What strengths do I have? (List them)

   b Are there some strengths which more frequently account for my successes than others?

   c. What limitations handicap me in things I want to do?

   d. Do certain limitations interfere more often than others?

PERSONAL ACHIEVEMENTS AND DISAPPOINTMENTS

Below, check personal resources and abilities that apply to each experience.	ACCOMPLISHMENTS					DISAPPOINTMENTS				
	1	2	3	4	5	1	2	3	4	5
A. USING SPIRITUAL RESOURCES										
1. Knowing the Word and power of God										
2. Applying the power of prayer										
3. Faith										
4. Drawing upon the inspiration & support of fellow Christians										
5. Other (Be specific)										
B. USING MY HANDS										
6. Assembling										
7. Constructing or building										
8. Operating tools										
9. Machinery										
10. Showing manual or finger dexterity										
11. Handling with precision and/or speed										
12. Fixing or repairing										
13. Other (Be specific)										

PERSONAL ACHIEVEMENTS AND DISAPPOINTMENTS

Below, check personal resources and abilities that apply to each experience.

	ACCOMPLISHMENTS					DISAPPOINTMENTS				
	1	2	3	4	5	1	2	3	4	5
C. USING MY BODY										
14. Muscular coordination										
15. Doing outdoor activities										
16. Other (Be specific)										
D. USING WORDS										
17. Reading										
18. Copying										
19. Communicating through writing										
20. Talking or speaking										
21. Teaching, training										
22. Editing										
23. Memory for words (people's names, book titles, etc.)										
24. Other (Be specific)										
E. USING MY SENSES (Eyes, ears, nose, taste or touch)										
25. Observing, surveying										

PERSONAL ACHIEVEMENTS AND DISAPPOINTMENTS

Below, check personal resources and abilities that apply to each experience.	ACCOMPLISHMENTS					DISAPPOINTMENTS				
	1	2	3	4	5	1	2	3	4	5
26. Diagnosing, determining										
27. Showing attention to detail										
28. Other (Be specific)										
F. USING NUMBERS										
29. Taking inventory										
30. Counting										
31. Calculating, computing										
32. Keeping financial records, bookkeeping										
33. Managing Money										
34. Developing a budget										
35. Number memory										
36. Rapid manipulation of numbers										
37. Other (Be specific)										
G. USING INTUITION										
38. Showing foresight (as in planning ahead)										

PERSONAL ACHIEVEMENTS AND DISAPPOINTMENTS

	ACCOMPLISHMENTS					DISAPPOINTMENTS				
Below, check personal resources and abilities that apply to each experience.	1	2	3	4	5	1	2	3	4	5
39. Quickly sizing up a person or situation accurately										
40. Having insight (as to why people act as they do)										
41. Ability to visualize (as in drawings, models, blueprints, etc.)										
42. Other (Be specific)										
H. USING ANALYTICAL THINKING OR LOGIC										
43. Researching, information gathering										
44. Analyzing, dissecting										
45. Organizing, classifying										
46. Problem-solving										
47. Separating important from unimportant										
48. Diagnosing										
49. Systematizing, putting things in order										
50. Comparing, perceiving similarities and differences										
51. Testing, screening										
52. Reviewing, evaluating										

PERSONAL ACHIEVEMENTS AND DISAPPOINTMENTS

	ACCOMPLISHMENTS					DISAPPOINTMENTS				
	1	2	3	4	5	1	2	3	4	5
Below, check personal resources and abilities that apply to each experience.										
53. Other (Be specific)										
I. USING ORIGINALITY OR CREATIVITY										
54. Imaginative, imagining (as in figuring out new ways to do things)										
55. Inventing, creating										
56. Designing, developing										
57. Improvising										
58. Adapting, improving (as with something that doesn't work quite right)										
59. Other (Be specific)										
J. BEING HELPFUL										
60. Helping, being of service (as when someone is in need)										
61. Showing sensitivity to others' feelings										
62. Listening										
63. Developing rapport (as with someone who is initially a stranger, etc.)										
64. Conveying warmth, caring										
65. Understanding										

PERSONAL ACHIEVEMENTS AND DISAPPOINTMENTS

Below, check personal resources and abilities that apply to each experience.	ACCOMPLISHMENTS					DISAPPOINTMENTS				
	1	2	3	4	5	1	2	3	4	5
66. Drawing out people										
67. Offering support (as when someone is facing a difficulty alone)										
68. Motivating others to act or change										
69. Sharing credit, appreciation										
70. Making others feel better about themselves										
71. Counseling, guiding										
72. Other (Be specific)										
K. USING ARTISTIC ABILITIES										
73. Composing music										
74. Playing (a) musical instrument(s), singing										
75. Fashioning or shaping things, materials										
76. Dealing creatively with symbols or images										
77. Dealing creatively with spaces, shapes or faces										
78. Dealing creatively with colors										
79. Conveying feelings and thoughts (as in acting, public speaking)										

PERSONAL ACHIEVEMENTS AND DISAPPOINTMENTS

	ACCOMPLISHMENTS					DISAPPOINTMENTS				
Below, check personal resources and abilities that apply to each experience.	1	2	3	4	5	1	2	3	4	5
80. Conveying feelings and thoughts through drawing, painting, etc.)										
81. Using words (as in poetry, novels, etc.)										
82. Other (Be specific)										
L. USING LEADERSHIP, BEING UP FRONT										
83. Beginning new tasks: starting a group, clothing drive, etc.										
84. Initiating relationships with strangers in Church, on bus, etc.)										
85. Organizing projects and people										
86. Leading, directing others										
87. Promoting change (as in a family, community, organizations)										
88. Making decisions (as in places where decisions affect others, etc.)										
89. Taking risks (as in supporting an unpopular decision)										
90. Getting up before a group, (performing, teaching, demonstrating, etc.)										
91. Selling, promoting, negotiating, persuading										
92. Other (Be specific)										

PERSONAL ACHIEVEMENTS AND DISAPPOINTMENTS

	ACCOMPLISHMENTS					DISAPPOINTMENTS				
Below, check personal resources and abilities that apply to each experience.	1	2	3	4	5	1	2	3	4	5
M. USING FOLLOW-THROUGH										
93. Using what others have developed										
94. Following-through on instructions, plans										
95. Attending to details										
96. Classifying, recording, filing, retrieving										
97. Other (Be specific)										

When inventorying your strengths and limitations, you have no doubt already thought of other uses that can be made of this information. Some of your strengths may serve as the basis for new goals. For example, you may have found new and better ways to serve the Lord by utilizing skills or gifts in your church or community. You may also have thought of ways in which your strengths can help you better achieve goals you already have.

The resources and limitations you have identified may also be useful in your decision-making process. They can help you determine:

1. Which options (courses of action) may be particularly strenghthened by the personal resources you can bring to them.

2. What deficiencies present a serious handicap to the success of possible involvements.

SUMMARY

We can achieve personal integrity, or "wholeness," when we understand our God-given purpose in life, recognize what our values are and express them in personal, long range goals and short range, measurable objectives. Personal fulfillment will become possible as we enter every decision-making situation with these clearly in mind. The self-inventory process becomes a discovery of personal resources and limitations that helps us make decisions with greater assurance that they fit into God's plan for us, since He made us able to assume personal responsibility.

Section II

A SEVEN STEP PLAN
THAT WORKS

A SEVEN STEP PLAN THAT WORKS

Doug and Sherry faced a complicated decision that not only affected them individually, but also their children. Doug might achieve his career goals by the move, and Sherry might actually move into a whole new world of arts and crafts. Yet what could the move do for their children's educational goals, for them spiritually. The move could seriously limit vocational options. How could Doug and Sherry get all of these, and many other, factors into the decision-making mix and still come up thinking straight?

In the first two chapters we have established the larger framework for decision-making—our relationship to God and His purpose for us as expressed in the Bible. We outlined some of the factors that affect decision-making, that result in indecisiveness. Acknowledging that all of us want to feel part of a larger purpose, we established that this can be found in gaining a clearer understanding of who we are and what we can achieve as servants of Jesus Christ. Our uniqueness is an expression of the diversity of God's creation, but we sometimes need help to determine where we fit in. That's why we set up the analysis of strengths and weaknesses. If you have not done that exercise, please do so before you proceed, because this understanding of yourself is critical to the decisions you may be working through as you read this book.

With all of this information as our frame of reference, we can now introduce a seven step decision-making process that has been tested over and over again and proved highly workable. You can use it for the so-called minor decisions in an abbreviated form, but you will want to apply each procedure much more fully in the more complex personal and group decisions in which you will be involved. These seven steps will help you avoid the "oops, I forgot that" syndrome. But they will also prevent you from jumping ahead of yourself and making a decision you may truly regret.

Here are the seven steps:

1. *Determine the Issues.* In other words, why do I have to make a decision?

2. *State Your Purpose.* What is it that I am really trying to determine?

3. *Set Up Standards for Evaluating Alternatives.* What do I want to achieve, preserve, or avoid?

4. *Establish Your Priorities.* What conditions and personal goals *must* be met by my decision, and which are desirable but not mandatory?

5. *Search for Solutions.* What alternatives might meet the standards I have established?

6. *Test the Alternatives.* Which alternatives best fit my priorities and standards/criteria?

7. *Troubleshoot Your Decision.* Is there anything that could go wrong?

By now you may be saying, "Wow, do you really have to make decision-making so complicated?" You may feel that the pros and cons approach of Doug and Sherry is more your speed. Yet these seven steps are not as complicated as they may seem when stated all together. In fact, they really do simplify the process, taking a lot of the emotional heat out of decision-making.

Suppose you just bought your son a train set, or yourself a new grill for barbecuing. You get everything out of the box and start assembling the pieces. About halfway through you are ready to throw something (unless you happen to be a mechanical genius), when suddenly you discover the directions. *Voila,* suddenly everything starts to make sense, and even you can do it. That's how you will feel about the decision-making process we will describe for you in greater detail in the next few chapters.

You see, each of the steps is actually a logical reflection of how people think. Most people have already used every step of this process at one time or another without being aware of it. In fact, you may very well be saying, "That's right. I've tried all of that, and it did not work." If that's the case, then it is likely you did not follow through the process in the sequence we have described.

We would not have dared put this decision-making process on paper without having trained thousands of people in this system and getting back their enthusiastic report, "It works!"

You are one of those who doesn't have time "for one of those fancy processes"? You've got work to do and "can't play around"? Ever consider how costly a bad decision can be, how much work it can create for you that you could have avoided?

One of the companies we know was growing tremendously. The future looked great! The president decided that the company could easily start two new divisions with existing manpower and expertise. Within two years the treasurer began complaining about cash flow, even though the new divisions appeared to be on the road to success. The president assured him that everything would be okay, the new divisions would be showing a profit soon. Unfortunately, the economy slowed down just at that time. The new divisions did not become profitable, and the established divisions declined in profitability. Suddenly the cash flow problem became critical.

What had gone wrong? In the first place, the president had not asked himself, "What do I want to achieve, preserve or avoid?" Because of that he had never asked for a financial study focusing on the impact of inventory buildup. Secondly, he had not asked, "What could go wrong?" and thus had not counted on the decline in the economy. The euphoria of success had carried away even this trained accountant and management specialist.

You're not going to make that kind of a mistake? Don't count on it. That's why we will "walk" you through numerous examples of decision-making as we describe the seven steps that will make you a successful decision-maker. By the time you will have worked through the rest of this book you will have the process firmly in your head and part of your thinking processes.

Chapter 3

Do I Need To Make a Decision?

STEP ONE

"I went into our teenage daughter's room this morning and discovered another body sleeping in one of the beds," reported Ann as she settled in for another day at the office. "I asked my daughter who this was, and she reported that it was a friend from school."

Ann slipped a letterhead into her typewriter.

"Can she stay, for a couple of days, Mom?" her daughter had pled. "Her Mom beats her, and she just can't take it anymore," Ann reported as her typewriter went into action.

Already close to being late for work, Ann had felt she could not take the time to discuss everything needed to make a decision. So she had said, "Let's talk about it tonight."

Early afternoon the telephone rang on Ann's desk. Picking it up she heard her teen daughter's voice saying, "You won't need to worry about us for supper. Sylvia and I are getting a bite at McDonald's and then going to a movie."

"But you must be in by midnight," Ann quickly said, injecting the only cautionary note she could think of at the moment. She was too preoccupied with the job in her typewriter to make any decisions about her daughter's activity, so she simply accepted what was happening.

That night Ann could not fall asleep. As she tossed restlessly in bed the clock struck twelve, then one, two, and finally three. At that point the headlights of a car swung onto the driveway. When the car door opened, a strange young woman struggled out of the car and headed unsteadily for the front door. Ann watched in growing fear, for the car drove off without leaving her daughter. At the moment she knew that not making a decision that morning had been a decision—and had resulted in decisions over which she had no control.

What had put Ann in this unenviable position? She had been faced with a situation that required some time to smoke out the issues, to determine what was really happening, and what was at stake for the future, and she had felt that getting to the office on time was more important. Time not taken to make a decision had given her sleepless hours and a new problem.

What happens when you do make a decision? Let me suggest several things that happen:

1. You invest your own time and effort, and possibly that of others as well.

2. You commit material resources (money, space, equipment).

3. You affect how others feel about you. Put another way, your self-image and reputation are affected, negatively or positively.

4. You either expand or decrease future options.

There are, of course, times when a decision is not necessary, and making one without determining the necessity for that decision can have serious negative effects. Doing nothing would have been more helpful!

Consider the father whose son attended a private secondary school. Recognizing the financial burden the tuition and board and room put on his parents, the son applied himself diligently to his studies. He also participated extensively and successfully in the sports and music program, ultimately receiving the school's highest award for dedication and citizenship. During the summer he worked to help defray the school expenses.

The proud father told his son that he could choose a college without worrying about cost. Since the father had recently received a substantial increase in salary he felt reasonably confident that finances would be no problem.

The son selected a university with an outstanding program in his field of study, even though it meant traveling 1,000 miles one way and paying exceptionally high tuition. After the first semester the son complained that the noise and activity in the dormitories made study practically impossible. He asked if he could join a fraternity house which offered more quiet (on class nights at least). He promised to find summer work and earn the additional several hundred dollars needed to cover fraternity fees.

During his freshman year the son came home for both the Christmas vacation and the summer recess. Both times he took a job with a landscape architect. As a result he covered the additional expenses of the fraternity house and was also able to buy a used car.

As he approached the second year the son found that tuition costs could be significantly reduced by taking some of the basic courses he needed at a nearby university. His advisors approved his plan, and he was even able to continue living at the fraternity house. So he registered at the neighboring university, now accessible because he had his own car. Yet when he tried to sign up for the classes he needed, he discovered that they were all full and he would have to wait for the next semester. Since it was now too late to register at his own school, he was unable to attend any classes. He decided to stay on, work a semester, and try again. Yet the part-time job he found barely paid for his living expenses. This did not worry him, however, for his father had assured him when he started college that tuition was not a problem.

Unfortunately, the family had meanwhile experienced a significant increase in expenses, including a substantial increase in real estate taxes. With the rapidly escalating tuition at the son's school, the father realized he would be unable to keep his commitment. Finally he had to communicate this to his son, resulting in a most awkward relationship.

Could this have been avoided? Did the father really have to decide to give his son full support at college? The son had been more than willing to work hard and contribute to expenses for a private high school, and probably would have been glad to help with college fees. He certainly did not ask his father to make so heavy a commitment. Yet because of the father's decision he is now depressed and angry with himself, and the son is perplexed and disappointed. The father made a decision he did not have to make.

Okay, when do you know that a decision is necessary? We have found the following guidelines most helpful:

A decision is necessary when

1. Something has happened that should not have happened, and needs to be *corrected*.

2. Something can happen that you do not want to happen, and needs to be *prevented*.

3. Something you want to happen is *not* happening, and *needs to happen*.

4. Something is missing, and *needs to be provided*.

Test these guidelines against the example of the mother with a stranger in her daughter's bedroom, against the father seeing his son off to college, and against the earlier illustration of Doug and Sherry.

Having indicated the importance of determining whether a decision needs to be made, and the criteria to apply to situations that come to our attention, we can move to a discussion of the first of the seven steps in decision-making: *determine the issues*. When you have done that, it is much easier to define your problem and aim your decision at the right target.

You would think this is so basic that it would be quickly apparent to anyone facing a decision. Not so, for very few of us learned even that basic step in any of the courses we took. Nor do we have supervisors who model this approach to decision-making.

Consider the crisis experienced by one of the major automobile companies during a recent recession. To compete with imports, the corporation designed and built a highly-automated plant to manufacture compacts. To reduce costs, workers on the assembly line were assigned additional tasks at their work stations. Work studies had shown that these extra assignments could be done with little difficulty before the automobile moved onto the next work station. This redistribution of work made some workers redundant and they were laid off.

Workers in this plant soon began slow-down tactics. Among

other actions, they let body and engine units go by their work stations without completing all their assigned tasks—or none at all. Even the addition of supervisors to these assembly lines did not stop the violators. Management's next move was to stop the lines on which these work infractions occurred and send the workers home. Since they were hourly workers, this hit the workers hard financially. Many were married, had young families, and new mortgages. Yet when the assembly lines were re-started, the slow-down continued. There were even cases of mild sabotage, with Coca Cola bottles welded into the frames of cars and countless nuts put into hubcaps.

Soon the parking area for completed cars was filled with cars returned by dealers because of defects. And after several months of such disruptive action, the workers went out on strike, shutting down the plant.

What had happened? By all indications, the management had failed to determine what the real issues were, they had failed to "smoke" out the issues.

Remember Nehemiah? He was discussing the state of the city of Jerusalem one day with some travelers and realized how badly it needed a new wall to protect its residents from marauding bands. He "asked them concerning the Jews that had escaped, which were left of the captivity, and concerning Jerusalem" (Nehemiah 1:2). Once he had determined the issues, he was ready to plead with the king for a "sabbatical" so he could journey to Jerusalem and provide leadership in rebuilding the walls. When he got there he again set out to determine the facts of the situation by riding around the city.

In chapter five, Nehemiah is told about the corruption and social injustices. Again he takes time to determine what has been happening before he acts. Before he made any decision he determined what was at stake.

Some time ago a teacher friend called us, her voice betraying real agitation.

"I'm really upset over returning to teaching at the end of the summer, and I just don't know what to do. I'd like to discuss it with you. Could you and your wife come over this evening and help me decide what to do?"

Knowing that the question "why" is most effective in getting at the heart of the issue, I asked her, "Why are you upset, Jackie?"

"I just feel that I'm working with people who do not understand what I'm doing. I know more about my area of specialization than they do," she responded. Thus far she had not given me a real reason for making any decision, so I returned to a "why" question.

"Why do you need to do anything?"

Her answer revealed that she wanted to *prevent* something from happening: "I'm so frustrated and angry that I'm afraid that when I get back to school, I'll lose my temper and really foul things up."

Since her anger was clearly directed at people rather than specific policies, I turned to a second effective question, the *what* question.

"What people are we talking about?"

"The business manager, the superintendent, the head of the department," she said.

"Okay, give us an hour. We'll be over," I told her, recognizing that we would need more time to get at some deep-rooted issues.

This friend is a special teacher in a fairly large school system. She has taught for several years in this particular system, moving about from school to school because of her specialized classes. Recently there were several administrative personnel changes, and these were clearly the cause of her distress.

Once we were comfortably seated in her living room I resumed the *why* line of questioning.

"Jackie, why do you feel that the business manager, the superintendent, and the department head don't understand what you're doing?"

"I'm on the bottom of the priority list. I can't get what I need to do the things that need to be done, that I need to do if I'm really going to do an effective job of teaching."

Clearly, it was time for some specifics, so I returned to the *what* question.

"What happened that shouldn't have happened?"

"Okay. Last spring I put in a requisition for a special piece of stationery equipment that I use in my teaching and that I have in the classrooms of all the other schools. It costs two hundred dollars, but I had the money in my budget so I sent in the requisition to the business manager, with copies to my department head and the superintendent, as we're supposed to do. I had discussed with my department head why I needed it, and he did not seem to have any objection. I waited several weeks for approval, then inquired about it. I was told they were working on it. I still did not have it by the end of the school year. Just yesterday I received a letter from the superintendent's office telling me that the business manager wants to discuss my requisition with me. I know he's going to tell me I can't have the piece of equipment I need."

She was clearly feeling rather sorry for herself, so I tried to get her to rethink what had happened.

"Whoa, Jackie, just a minute. Have you explained why you need it to the business manager?"

"I explained it to my department head. The trouble is they don't understand what I'm doing—and furthermore, they don't care!"

Her emotional reaction to the situation seemed to be obscuring some of the positive factors. An excellent way to defuse emotional anger is to insert a non-accusatory question.

"*Is it possible* that you are assuming some things that may not be true? For example, aren't you *assuming* that your department head has discussed your reasons for the requisition with the business manager? Since you already had it in your budget, he may not have seen any reason for discussing it with him unless he was asked about it. And aren't you *assuming* that the business manager's purpose in meeting with you is to turn down your requisition?"

I could see some doubt arising as she responded, "Yes, I guess I am."

Remember the criterion for when a decision is necessary? Try to catch it in the next question I asked her.

"*What* do you want to happen that *isn't* happening?"

"I want to get approval to purchase that piece of equipment."

"Okay, let's go to work on that," I told her.

Let's briefly review the questions that helped to determine

the issues, to clarify the situation requiring a decision:

1. A key question is "why?" Ask it repeatedly: "Why do you need to make a decision? Why do you need to do anything? Why do you feel that way?"

2. The second important question is "what?" What happened that shouldn't have happened? What have you seen that indicates that? What people are we talking about? What do you want to happen that isn't happening? What could happen that you need to prevent? What are you assuming that may not be true?

These questions are like surgical tools that help you get at the heart of the matter. They are not hard to use, but they do require discipline and persistence.

Up to this point each illustration has focused on only one concern. What can you do when several concerns hit you at once? How do you determine which to work on first?

Nehemiah faced that kind of situation, although a reading of the first chapters does not reveal this because of his single-minded devotion to rebuilding the wall. Yet he also faced a corrupt society with many injustices. The Sabbath was being violated. Racial intermarriage contrary to Mosaic law made ethnic purity impossible. Why did he tackle rebuilding the wall first? Clearly, he established a priority list, focusing on what had to be done immediately, what could wait for the wall to be built, and what could only be taken care of in a more stable society possible when the people felt secure.

Consider a contemporary counterpart. You are at a church council meeting. By the time you are forty minutes into the agenda you realize you have six issues requiring attention and action:

1. The church building committee has asked for church council approval of funds to make major repairs on the church roof. During a heavy storm the previous week, water leaked into the organ loft.

2. The council has been asked to discuss whether a new position of assistant pastor should be established, with basic responsibilities for youth programs. An excellent candidate, a seminary graduate, is available.

3. The National Church Conference is a month away, and delegates must be selected for that.

4. The pastor has received a letter from a newly-formed Alcohol Anonymous group asking whether they could use the social hall for their meetings.

5. The superintendent of the Sunday school has requested permission to purchase a "good" piano.

6. The church has received a request for an additional contribution to support missionary work in Kenya.

Unless members stay until midnight, it is highly unlikely that the council can devote adequate attention to each of the six items. What criteria can help the council determine which issues deserve priority?

If you are an experienced church council member you may well have identified at least one useful criteria for establishing what the top issues are:

1. How *urgent* is it that a decision be made? How soon *must* action be taken? Can it wait a few days? A week? A month? Or do we actually have to make a decision?

We have found a second guideline very helpful:

2. What *impact* is the situation having? What effect is the situation having on fulfilling the principal purpose of the church? What would happen if you do not do anything about it?

A third question has also proved helpful:

3. Does the council actually have control over this? Are we able to do anything about it?

Every issue has a certain amount of emotional attachment by various members of the council. For that reason something very important in our mind may not seem as important to the whole council. That's why we will need to provide factual, objective information that clearly indicates that something *must* be done about it *now*. Conversely, we can willingly and even enthusiastically commit ourselves to working on another issue when the facts tell us that issue is much more critical than ours. The criteria questions suggested help to establish the facts needed to set up priorities, enabling the group to efficiently direct its energy and resources.

Let's get back to the six issues facing the church council. Since roof repairs are needed immediately to *prevent* more damage to the organ, a valuable instrument, this agenda item clearly has the greatest urgency. If that is all that the council gets to on this particular evening, it will have tackled the only problem with insistent urgency.

There is clearly also some deadline on the availability of the candidate for the assistant pastor position. Unless action is taken within a reasonable time, he may take on another assignment. Because of the effect on the budget, only approval in principle can be given, with a request to the finance committee to establish whether funds will be available long term.

The church conference also has a deadline—it is a month away. Since delegate selection is usually only a perfunctory item this could be slipped in between major items.

The three other requests can easily be deferred to another meeting. In most cases they have been waiting for action for some time anyway!

Let us return to Doug and Sherry and the possibility of a move to New Hampshire as part of a promotion. What are the issues that need to be put on the table as the first step in the decision-making process? Here are some questions designed to reveal the true issues.

1. What do we want to happen that isn't happening? Is it a promotion? A change in lifestyle?

2. What is happening that should not be happening? Is the lack of movement up the corporate ladder frustrating Doug?

3. What is likely to happen if we do not take any action? Will that mean that Doug will be pigeonholed as "not promotable"?

Since many of our decisions have to be made in a group setting, we are now introducing an actual experience involving one of the authors. We will refer back to this repeatedly as a parallel experience to that of Doug and Sherry.

One of the authors has for several years served as president of the board of directors of a crisis intervention center. This social agency has been in existence for more than ten years and serves a wide variety of community needs. Included in these services are a 24-hour-a-day emergency telephone counseling service manned by trained volunteers; a foster parent program; an adolescent and family counseling service; an outward-bound type of program involving hiking, canoeing, and skiing for pre-teen and teen street kids; a drug treatment facility. All involve some level of participation by paid staff, who, along with the volunteers, tend to be younger people in their twenties or early thirties because they relate more easily to hostile "acting out" youth. The agency is funded by several municipal, state, and federal grants which are awarded on an annual basis.

One day the president received a call from the capable young executive-director that began with, "I've got a problem. . . . " Seems there had been an evening party given for staff, volunteers, and their wives the previous week. Usually these annual parties were held outside, but this time it was held in the administrative offices on the first floor of the building occupied by the agency. The executive-director had given firm instructions that the party was to be confined to the first floor, with no one to interfere with the counseling going on by hotline volunteers.

After the party was over, the executive-director received a call from someone working in the agency, reporting that a staff member and a volunteer had left the party, gone outside, taken some marijuana from one of the cars and gone upstairs to the telephone room. There they lit up. They were briefly joined by the telephone counselor and one other volunteer. Still later, a staff member came upstairs, took one puff, and said, "This is ridiculous! We shouldn't be doing this!" He immediately left the building. That particular person had been doing an outstanding job in starting, developing, and supervising a major new program in the agency for which it had been very difficult to find a qualified candidate.

Everyone knew that the agency had an explicit policy prohibiting bringing illicit drugs into the building. At the weekly staff conference, knowing that other people than agency personnel would be at the party, the executive-director had again forcefully repeated the prohibition.

After the executive-director had given the details of the incident, he asked the president, "What do *you* think we should do about these people?"

Consider the question we asked at the start of this chapter: "Is a decision necessary? If so, what are the issues?" Jot down some answers for yourself before moving on to the the next chapter.

Chapter 4

What's to Decide?

STEP TWO

Ever feel you have to make a decision because you have been backed into a corner? A quick survey of the options reveals that none is attractive enough for you to go for it unhesitatingly. Or you have to make a decision with a deadline on it, and you cannot seem to get clear guidance from the Holy Spirit. Often the necessity to make a decision can so paralyze us emotionally that we need help.

Up to now we have covered how to determine if you really need to make a decision—and how to determine what the issues really are. This chapter will give you a central focus, the statement of purpose for that decision, to help you make another step forward in the decision-making process.

Let's think of Doug and Sherry again. Doug has been offered a promotion that will involve a move from California to New Hampshire. He is concerned not only about his climb up the executive ladder but also the impact a move would have on his wife and children. *What really has to be decided?*

As Doug and Sherry sit down to consider this question of purpose in their decision-making their writing pad may look something like this:

"Determine the best way to fulfill my (Doug's) responsibilities to the Lord and my family."

Notice how putting down a statement of purpose moves the focus away from merely accepting a promotion or not? Even though this may initially seem to add complicating factors to the decision, the process will give you a much better feeling about the decision later. It could, in fact, enhance the family's experience even if Doug and Sherry decide to stay put.

Another example will help to clarify what a statement of purpose can do for the decision-making process. Imagine yourself on the church council of a small rural church in Wisconsin. In early September the temperature suddenly drops and the oil burner has to go on for the first time in months. The burner has provided years of service, but the boiler is now rusting and has already been patched several times. Thus when the thermostat signaled time for start-up, the burner started up dutifully. Yet oily smoke also began pouring out through some new holes in the boiler, so that by the time the custodian arrived next morning an oily film covered the interior of the church. Smoke continued to pour from the furnace, billowing up the stairs into the sanctuary until the burner was shut off.

The custodian called the minister, who quickly recognized that the risk of repairing the old boiler was too great. He called together the church council, since they would have to authorize any action.

What has to be decided?

The statement of what has to be determined could take several forms. Which of the following two statements, in your opinion, best represents the decision to be made?

1. Select the best oil burner and boiler.
2. Determine the best way to heat the church.

Ready for a little self-analysis? First ask yourself why you selected the statement you did. Does it really make any difference which statement you choose? Will the focus of discussion on the church council be any different if it decides the first statement is its statement of purpose rather than the second? Which statement allows you to consider more options in reaching a final choice? How important is it that you have more options to choose from?

The pressure to "make a decision" in situations such as the above frequently produces tunnel vision. People, without realizing it, confine themselves to a very narrow range of actions in reaching their decision. An example would be if the church council felt that its only decision was, "Do we buy a new furnace or don't we—yes or no?" They would still be limiting their options unnecessarily if they simply asked, "Do we replace our bad furnace with a Type A furnace or a Type B furnace?" With oil shortages a recurring phenomenon, why limit the option to oil furnaces?

Stu was thinking about purchasing a vehicle. He had a large family that enjoyed camping, so he felt that his decision was simply, "Select the best station wagon." Yet this "tunnel vision" eliminated consideration on a number of other possibilities, including vans, recreational vehicles, or even a truck with a camper on it. These options would have remained open if he had stated as the purpose of his decision, "Determine the best way to provide family transportation."

By now you will have realized that it is often better to develop *more* rather than fewer alternatives. For this reason it is necessary to define the purpose of the decision more broadly to avoid accidentally excluding excellent alternatives. As we expand the number of possible solutions there is greater likelihood of finding one suited to our needs.

Let's go back to the furnace problem in Wisconsin. Given the concerns about the future availability and cost of fuel oil, it seems likely that the church council ought to state as its purpose, "Find the best way to heat the church." This makes it possible to consider alternate sources of fuel, such as wood, coal, natural gas, and combinations of such fuels.

Earlier we took a look at Doug and Sherry's statement of purpose. If they had restricted their purpose for decision-making to what was on Doug's mind when he came home it would have read, "To decide whether we should accept the promotion and move to New Hampshire." Yet when he and Sherry opened their mind to some of the larger purposes of their life together as a family, they realized that moving to New Hampshire was not the only way to achieve their purposes individually and as a family.

Our work as decision process consultants brought us into contact with a young, vigorous company president who in a little over ten years had taken his company from a two-man operation to annual sales of more than $5.5 million. Employees now totaled more than 200. To strenghten growth potential, he had recently purchased another company that was not yet providing an adequate return on investment. He had also purchased some sophisticated and expensive equipment for the company. Suddenly the capital resources of the company were gone, just when he needed capital to install a much-needed computer system. In vain he approached several commercial banks and venture companies for financing. The very day we met with him his vice-president of finance informed him that the company would not be able to meet the payroll in three months if something was not done.

The young president confessed that the stresses of trying to keep his growing company afloat were now being exasperated by conditions at home. He had put so much time into building up the company that he had neglected relationships at home. Conditions were reaching a crisis point at the same time as the company crisis. Obviously he had to "do something" or he would have an emotional breakdown.

We sat down to begin the decision-making process. Initially he saw as the purpose of the decision-making process, "Determine whether or not to sell the business." We continued the analysis of the issues, and he highlighted several of his personal values. These led to a more panoramic view of the crises and he was able to redefine the purpose of the decision as, "Determine the best way to bring my spiritual, business, and family life into proper balance." This broadening of purpose opened up a much wider range of options: selling the company but remaining as president; selling and leaving the company, but retaining partial ownership; selling the company and using some of the proceeds in a joint business venture with his wife; and *not* selling the company, but rather bringing in outside help to assist him in solving the critical problems facing him. This outside help might also be used to help strengthen family relationships, and establish Bible study patterns.

Nehemiah, like Doug and Sherry, received news that led to a major life-changing decision. What might he have put down as concerns? Taking our cues from verses two and three of chapter one, here are concerns he may have listed:

1. To provide relief for the distressed remnant left in Jerusalem.

2. To restore Jerusalem to its former glory as a capital city.

3. To provide a system of security against the marauding bands.

4. To build a wall around the ancient city of Jerusalem so people can resume normal life patterns.

Yet when you read to the end of the chapter you suddenly realize that Nehemiah's concern is much wider. He is deeply concerned about the spiritual condition of the remnant, confessing that they had sinned against God and need spiritual healing. He reminds God that, "Now these are thy servants and thy people, whom thou hast redeemed by thy great power, and by the strong hand" (verse 10). So we could identify his *purpose* as: To provide the kind of environment that will make possible the spiritual revitalization of those still living in Jerusalem.

Nehemiah thus arrived in Jerusalem with a wide variety of options, with enablements in the form of letters from his sovereign. His first ride around the burned out city, with its broken down walls, quickly convinced him that until the people had a wall that guranteed security nothing much else could happen. His purpose had informed his decision on solutions.

That this statement of purpose can be extremely valuable in directing how you will evaluate possible solutions later on is illustrated by the experience of a church music committee. The pastor gave the committee what at first glance is a rather straightforward assignment: "Find a replacement for our church choir director." Without too much decision-making effort, the committee could have stated the purpose as: "Select the best replacement for the choir director."

This committee, however, took some time to consider what really had to be decided, and why. They arrived at a much more significant and far-reaching purpose: "Determine the best way to ensure spiritual growth through music." You see, spiritual growth was an important Christian goal for the members of this committee, and its inclusion in the purpose for the decision added a dimension that could have been overlooked in the evaluation of candidates. The upshot was that the candidates were not only questioned regarding their credentials and experience in music, but each was also carefully checked out on his or her spiritual goals through the ministry of music.

All this may seem like a rather mysterious way of broadening the purpose of a decision to appropriate limits. Be assured that this does not require extraordinary powers of "vision" or ability. You have already laid the foundation for a grasp of the "big picture" when you took the first step: determine the issues. The content and scope of the issues are the base upon which the purpose of the decision is built.

Before we illustrate how the issues are used in defining the purpose of the decision, let's first take another look at the term "appropriate broadening of the purpose." We use that term because it is important that the purpose be within the abilities and scope of the individual or group. The church music committee, for example, would exceed its assigned responsibility and capability if it tried to influence the content of the morning worship service other than music. The president facing the financial crisis in his company could hardly include in his purpose, "to strengthen the market penetration by expanding our sales force," since he was having difficulty paying the men he was now employing.

Yet the necessity to operate within the realm of the possible, and the ability to achieve the desired change, is not likely to handicap most decision-makers in their efforts to broaden the purpose of their decision. Our experience, rather, is that people tend to define their decisions too narrowly rather than too broadly. That being the case, how do we effectively establish what needs to be determined and state the purpose of such a decision?

Another example may help bring this into clearer focus. Our director of management services was conducting a management decision-making seminar with key managers of a company. They had delayed making a decision about an increasingly severe problem within their sales organizations and came prepared to implement the process described. When they were asked, "Why is any decision necessary?", the first step in the decision-making process, they revealed there were major discrepancies between the way their internal sales force and the way outside salesmen, independent manufacturer's representatives, were paid. Further probing brought out the following list of issues:

1. Internal company salesmen received base salaries plus a small commission on each sale. Outside manufacturer's representatives received a commission only, but it was substantial, providing them with greater incentive. Company salesmen resented their small commission.

2. Some manufacturer's representatives had been given territories that infringed on the sales territories of company salesmen.

3. Some manufacturer's representatives were angry over what they considered preferential treatment of other "outside" salesmen.

4. Some manufacturer's representatives were selling harder on items that were in their own best interests, but less profitable for the company.

5. Because the manufacturer's representatives were making these decisions, the company had lost control of what was being sold. Because of this the company at times had to manufacture products in quantities that were not profitable.

Asked, "What needs to be determined?" the managers said, "Determine how we can eliminate the disparity in compensation between the 'inside' and the 'outside' salesmen."

You be the judge at this point. Read over the five issues indentified to see if they could be resolved by a decision-making process with the purpose of "eliminating compensation disparities." Would doing this really solve all the problems highlighted?

Once it was confronted by these questions, the group quickly concluded that its initial purpose for the decision was not at all what had to be decided. Instead, they redefined it as, "Determine the best way to sell our products." Quite a change, isn't it? And what did this change in focus lead to? This new statement of purpose led to the consideration of options such as a totally internal sales force, a totally external sales organization, mail order sales, and several others that probably would not have emerged under the original purpose. Though these were intelligent managers they had lived with the problem for some years, always worried about the disparity in compensation and its effects on sales but unable to effectively tackle the issue until they had defined the broader purpose of the decision to be made.

Let's see how this insight can help in situations where anger, hurt, and disappointment may short-circuit sound decision-making. Consider the home in which parents of girls aged 14 and 16 went out for the evening, leaving the older in charge. Both girls knew that friends were not permitted in the house when the parents were not at home without the parents' prior consent. Yet when the parents returned home at midnight, they found cigarette butts and an empty carton of beer bottles that had apparently been hastily, but poorly, concealed. Asked if there had been any visitors, the older girl strongly denied it, bristling visibly at the hint that her parents did not trust her. Yet the younger sister later admitted that she had awakened and heard loud voices downstairs.

How would you have reacted? Naturally, you would have been terribly disappointed, since you probably had good reason to trust your children. Yet there was the evidence—and the confirmation from the younger sister. It is easy in such situations to "show who's boss around here," or set about "straightening her out."

These parents, aware of the steps in decision-making and disciplined in their reactions, took the time to reflect on what the real issues were. They determined that their purpose in deciding what to do about the situation was: "Determine the best way to ensure that she can be trusted in the future." This permitted them a much wider range of options in their response, allowing them to operate within a framework of unconditional love for their child while recognizing the severity of the transgression. It let them ask themselves, "What would Jesus do?" Instead of alienating a daughter they were able to effect repentance and initiate a new period of trust.

You may have noticed by now that many of our helpful statements of purpose begin with the words, "Determine the best way to. . . . " Try to make your statements *opportunity-*

oriented. In the case of the parents, "Punish her for breaking the rules" would have been one option, but it did not incorporate the opportunity for growth. "Ensure that she can be trusted in the future" is a much more positive, growth-oriented purpose.

We have let you participate in several decision-making statements of purpose. We conclude this chapter by involving you in the process we went through at the crisis intervention center, introduced in the last chapter. The following issues were pinpointed as a result of carefully analyzing that situation:

1. Two staff members acted in direct violation of the agency prohibition against bringing illicit drugs into the building.

2. Those two people, plus another staff member and a "telephone hotline" volunteer, participated at length in smoking marijuana in the telephone room.

3. One of the key staff members of the agency happened to come upon the scene, took one puff from a marijuana cigarette handed to him, and said to the other four, "This is ridiculous; we shouldn't be doing this," and left.

4. All five were in violation of a verbal directive at a staff meeting that there were to be "no drugs."

5. Knowledge of this episode by other social agencies and the police department could result in them stopping referrals to the agencies.

6. Knowledge of this episode by school officials in the area could very likely result in canceling the agency's counseling programs in the schools.

7. Should funding agencies learn of the incident, they could very easily withdraw program funds.

With these facts on the table, you determine WHAT SHOULD BE THE PURPOSE OF THE DECISION?

If you are like most of us, you are now facing a key decision. Take time now to write down the purpose of the decision. Only then should you go on to the next chapter.

Chapter 5

What Guides My Decisions?

STEP THREE

Kathi turned on the warming oven. She measured out the coffee and got the coffee-maker started. At that point the front door opened and she heard the steps of her husband.

"Welcome home," she called as she turned to greet his entry into the kitchen.

"Um-m-m, smells good. Are you about ready?" he said, sweeping her into his arms.

"You've got just enough time to get cleaned up," Kathi said.

Dan headed for the bathroom. Several minutes later he re-entered the kitchen, asking, "How'd the job hunt go today?"

"Do you need to ask? Can't you see I've slaved hours to get you a gourmet meal? You'll miss those if I get a job," she teased, although Dan sensed a serious undercurrent.

"Well, maybe I should learn to live without meals that add to my waist," he responded, not yet ready to wade into the heavy conversation he knew was coming.

As Dan pushed away his plate later on, he decided to get back to the topic he knew was uppermost in Kathi's mind.

"Kath, I ran across three questions today that might help you and me get a better fix on what you ought to be looking for," he said, putting his hand over hers. "Let me try them on you and see if they might help."

Kathi, desperate for any help in getting her mind in gear on a job, countered, "Okay, Mr. Manager, fire way."

Dan got up and rummaged in a drawer until he produced a sheet of paper and a pen. He sat down and wrote at the top, "What do I want to achieve?"

"Okay," he said, "tell me what you want to achieve by getting a job?"

Kathi took the pen and paper out of Dan's hand and looked at the question. Then she began to write:

1. Job satisfaction to replace the kind of satisfaction I had raising three children.

2. A position that will help me to grow.

3. A position that gives me enough income to make it worthwhile.

4. A job that will help me put to work some of the human relationship skills I have developed as a mother.

Dan interrupted her, "Stay broad enough so you can use these as a tape measure against the alternatives. Now let's move on to the second question."

Dan regained the paper and wrote down, "What do I want to preserve?"

"Think of the things you do not want to sacrifice because of a job," he said.

Kathi took the pen and again started writing.

1. A clean house. "I can't stand the idea of not having enough time to go through the house weekly with a vacuum, etc.," she said firmly.

2. Some time for myself so I can do some handcrafts.

3. Enough time to help out a neighbor in need.

4. Enough energy to sing in the church choir.

5. The ability to have an occasional party for friends.

"Are you starting to see a pattern developing?" Dan asked.

"What you're trying to tell me, " responded Kathi, "is that a fulltime job may not be what I want."

"I'll come back to that after you've answered my third question."

Dan wrote down, "What do you want to avoid in taking on a job?"

"That's easy," said Kathi, writing.

1. A treadmill that has me going morning to night, week in and week out, without a chance to get off and be refreshed.

2. A conflict with Dan's time at home, so we can enjoy each other now that the children are gone.

3. A job that requires Sunday morning work.

4. A job that makes it necessary for us to buy a new car.

"Great," Dan commented. "That provides some real help in considering the jobs available. It may mean a longer, possibly more tiring search, but you'll be happier with what you decide on."

At that point the telephone rang. It was for Kathi . . . and Dan knew it was time for a break. Maybe tomorrow she'd be ready to list the various alternatives available in the community.

You may not face exactly the kind of problem Dan and Kathi did, but the step they took is extremely important in any decision-making. If you've ever participated in a committee discussion that went round and round, with a good number of really great ideas, but never reached a conclusion, you will appreciate the "fix" these three questions help you to get on the issue to be decided.

Let's list the questions together so you can fix them in your mind. In fact, we suggest you memorize them right now so that as they come up again and again they simply deepen the memory roots!

1. What do you want to *achieve* by the decision you need to make?

2. What do you want to *preserve* by the decision you need to make?

3. What do you want to *avoid* by the decision you need to make?

Used carefully, these three questions can become the *criteria* by which you can develop, by contrasting and evaluating possible solutions. These *decision criteria* help you to incorporate your Christian principles and the biblical value system into your decision-making.

Consider the plight of Dick and Barbara. After twelve and

a half years of marriage a medical exam revealed a growth in her breast. Surgery revealed that only the growth needed to be removed, and for six months Barbara and Dick reveled in the knowledge that an early detection had prevented serious problems.

Then the growth recurred. When Barbara awoke from surgery this time she asked the nurse, "Is it gone?" The nurse knew exactly what Barbara meant and answered, "Yes," confirming Barbara's worst fears.

"I felt as though I were in hell, not in a swearing sense, but as though I were in a dark place," Barbara reported.

Dick was equally shocked and dumbfounded. He had been so sure the problem had been solved. Yet when the initial shock wave had passed, their faith in God rose to sustain them.

"I had always prided myself on being a positive person, and I couldn't go at this problem any other way. I don't think the good Lord is ready for me to die yet. After all, look at Job's experiences, and all the healing Christ did," Barbara said.

Yet difficult decisions had to be made during the time immediately after the surgery. All of their research revealed that the treatment for cancer was still very much a "hit and miss" method, a "trial and error process." Each treatment may or may not work. And as the cancer progessed, should artificial life support systems be used to keep her alive?

As Dick and Barbara faced the decisions they implicitly asked themselves, "What do we want to achieve by any action we take? What will it help us preserve? What do we think it will help us avoid?" Yet through it all she and Dick were guided by the principle, "Don't play God with yourself." For them, only God had the right to rule on her life and death.

Barbara made it past three "terminal" dates set by the doctors. Thirty days before she died she revealed one of the lessons learned through the most difficult years for her, Dick, and the children. She said, "There can be no rainbow without first the storm." The family had learned that it is in the storm that the colors of God's love, of the concern and love of friends, and the strength of a family united under God are most clearly shown. And the many decisions they had to make together had helped enrich those colors.

How Christian principles, established as one of the key criteria, can inform decision-making is also illustrated by the experience of a key executive in a medium-sized corporation. One of the principles he had determined to *preserve* was complete honesty in all actions. One day he was asked to decide what accounting procedures were to be followed regarding executive ownership of company-provided cars. He was pressured to apply certain accounting methods and reporting procedures that would enable the executives driving these automobiles to avoid some tax costs.

This executive did not have to spend a lot of time on decision-making when faced with the pressures. He saw the practices as "questionable" and thus failing to measure up to his criteria, "Complete honesty in all actions." And he remembered that even though this practice was not uncommon in other companies, the Apostle Paul had written, "For we dare not make ourselves of the number, or compare ourselves with some that commend themselves: but they measuring themselves by themselves, and comparing themselves among themselves, are not wise. But we will not boast of things without our measure, but according to the measure of the rule which God hath distributed to us, a measure to reach even unto you" (2 Corinthians 10:12-13). So he held firmly to his decision, despite the protests.

To his associates, the executive pointed out that the company required scrupulous honesty of its employees. Any deviation from this by the executives would certainly not be setting the right example. His decision held.

This example illustrates another important benefit of establishing clearly-defined criteria. By clearly designating "complete honesty" one of the criteria by which each possible solution would be judged, the executive was forced to thoroughly examine each alternative for any possible deviance or deception. Without that step, he might not have discovered the deceptiveness of the approach suggested by his own accounting department—or it may have been discovered only after it was approved and put into effect. Setting the criteria up front in the decision-making process permits your values to inform the decision-making.

Let's join Doug and Sherry as they take this step in the decision-making process regarding their move east and the opportunity for a promotion. Remember some of the purposes they put down for a decision? Let's consider how our three questions might help them if they selected as the purpose for Doug's decision: "Determine the best way to fulfill my responsibilities to the Lord and my family." Notice, the purpose has not been defined as "Decide whether or not to accept this job offer." Had that been his purpose, he might not have considered other opportunities and compared them with that offered by his company.

How did Doug develop his criteria—with a little help from Sherry? Let's repeat the question, "What is it I want to *achieve, preserve,* and *avoid* by any decision I make?" The following are reasonable criteria:

PURPOSE
Determine the best way to fulfill my responsibilities to the Lord and my family.

ACHIEVE
1. Interesting, exciting, and enjoyable work.
2. Good use of the skills and knowledge God has let me gain.
3. Personal growth and advancement within the company.
4. Compensation in keeping with my contribution.
5. Top management support of my efforts.
6. Flexibility to be actively involved in church work.
7. The opportunity to help others live more fulfilling lives.

PRESERVE
1. The quality of our family life and relationships.
2. My physical health.
3. Personal integrity on the job.
4. A lifestyle that glorifies our Savior.

AVOID
1. Interference with my participation in the church's activities.

2. Compromising my witness as a Christian.
3. Any situation where people do not seem committed to high quality in both product and service.

You will have noticed that these criteria represent a blend of spiritual, moral and material objectives. Our decision process can help you bring all three of these objectives into balance in the decisions you make.

In the previous chapter we alluded to the positive constructive result of pausing to reflect on the *real purpose* of a decision—especially when you are angry. The example was that of parental response to the daughter who permitted friends to visit her, contrary to parental instruction, when she was staying with a younger sister. Let's examine the decision criteria developed by these parents to illustrate how this third step in our ExecuTrak System can both suggest and expand the range of alternatives available.

PURPOSE OF THE DECISION
Determine the best way to ensure that our daughter can be trusted in the future.

ACHIEVE
Her honesty and forthrightness in the future.
Our mutual commitment to support the decision.
Her understanding that what she did was wrong.
Her understanding that we cannot accept this behavior.

PRESERVE
Her understanding that we love her unconditionally.

AVOID
Serious damage to our relationship with her.

Take time to re-read these criteria. What solutions come to mind that you might not have thought of if as a parent you did not have these criteria? How would you, for example, try to get across to her that you love her unconditionally even though you cannot accept the behavior of that evening? Would a rigid application of punishment achieve that goal? In chapter seven we will provide some help on using objectives to stimulate the search and development of innovative solutions.

Finally, we again return to the problem of the Crisis Intervention Center. The executive director and board president emphatically agreed that a decision had to be made. After some discussion they identified the purpose as: *Determine the best way to ensure the moral and professional integrity of the agency.* How does this compare with the purpose you identified at the end of the last chapter?

With the information gained in this chapter you can now move to the third step in the decision-making process regarding the center. Write down what you would want to *achieve, preserve,* and *avoid* by any action taken regarding the Crisis Intervention Center problem.

Summarizing, the basic reason for *developing your criteria* is to provide a *standard* from which to develop, and against which to evaluate, possible courses of action. When you do this, it helps you to focus your analysis against the backdrop of your spiritual, moral, and material concerns.

In the next chapter we will help you to use these criteria (what you want to achieve/preserve/avoid) as a screen against which to measure the alternative actions available to you. This will make it more likely that you will achieve the basic purpose of the decision-making process. You will be able to select that particular solution that better than any other satisfies the criteria you have set for yourself.

Chapter 6

What Are the Really Important Criteria?

STEP FOUR

Ever try to establish what are the most important elements in your decision-making? Just when you've decided achieving one goal is more important than preserving an already won advantage, you realize there is another goal gaining significance. There is a way out of this dilemma.

Let's recap what has happened with Doug and Sherry during their attempt to reach a decision regarding an opportunity for a promotion and a new challenge all the way across the continent. First they set out to determine what the real issue was, since they wanted to focus on the true issue to be resolved. As a second step they stated what the purpose of the decision was. In the third step they put down explicit statements about what they wanted to achieve, preserve, and avoid. These steps helped them bring the factors determining their final choice under their control, moving them further and further away from whim, chance, or the glib persuasions of others as determining factors in their decision process.

By now Doug and Sherry were aware that even though they would like to find an alternative that would, when acted upon, satisfy in full measure all they wished to achieve, preserve, and avoid, this was hardly likely. We live in an imperfect world as a result of man's fall into sin in the Garden of Eden, leaving perfection a relative thing until we get to heaven.

This is particularly true in today's world, where our ever-growing wants are having to be curbed by the reduced availability of resources. We are being forced to scale down our wants and focus on needs—and sometimes even those shrink under the onslaught of inflation.

There are also times when one criterion cannot be achieved without jeopardizing another. For example, attempting to improve the quality of a product may run up against a prohibitively high cost factor. For that reason, and because accomplishing any of the goals set in what we want to achieve, preserve, and avoid usually require some effort and cost, we need to determine which criteria are most important for us to gain satisfaction through our choice. To do that, we need a mechanism that helps us express relative differences in importance among the goals we have set down. This brings us to Step Four.

Establish Your Priorities

Of course, this is what some people attempt to do by listing pros and cons, just as Doug and Sherry did initially. Step Four, however, provides a more systematic way of doing it.

By now some reader is saying, "But where does this leave God in the decision-making process? Can't I depend on Him to speak to me directly somehow? You have it so systematized that decisions can be made without regard for God's will in my life." We grant that it is all too easy for us to set up techniques that shut out God. Yet we think you will agree that because we are fallible human beings we are so easily distracted by how we feel, by the seeming words of wisdom of various persuaders. They even influence us when we are in prayer.

The early church faced a major decision, described for us in Acts 15. Should new Christians from non-Jewish communities be forced into observing specific Jewish rites such as circumcision, or could the gospel do a truly new thing in new cultures? The decision was made only after hours of debate and discussion of what was really important for the Christian. When the leaders finally wrote the letter that the Apostle Paul carried with him to the new churches he had established, they wrote, "It seemed good unto us, being assembled with one accord . . . " and "It seemed good to the Holy Ghost, and to us. . . ." (Acts 15:25,28). What are they saying? It would appear that they considered their decision a meeting of minds informed by God through the Holy Spirit during the discussion of alternatives. The four items they felt necessary for all Christians to observe were the criteria finally coming out of the discussion.

The Apostle Peter set forth what he believed God wanted them to *achieve:* "that the Gentiles . . . should hear the word of the gospel, and believe" (Acts 15:7). Then he told those assembled what he believed they needed to *preserve;* "put no difference between us and them, purifying their hearts by faith" (v. 9). Finally, he established what should be *avoided;* "to put a yoke upon the neck of the disciples, which neither our fathers nor we were able to bear" (v. 10). That set the tone for the whole discussion, with Paul and Barnabas telling what God had achieved among the Gentiles, and James stating what he considered the absolutes.

Our steps in the decision-making process can similarly be informed of the Holy Spirit if you are open to His leading, asking Him for wisdom at each step. We believe this wisdom from God is particularly needed as you tackle Step Four: Establish Your Priorities.

From his work as a manager Doug was thoroughly acquainted with using a numerical system to establish relative significance of various factors. Evaluation sheets rating work performance often used this system. But he decided that Sherry, like many of us, might find it difficult to make that fine a judgment the first time through. Thus he initially made a "rough cut" of the criteria, using "very high," "high," "medium," and "low" to sort priorities among them. Here's what Doug eventually could show Sherry.

PURPOSE
   Determine the best way to fulfill my responsibilities to the Lord and my family.

ACHIEVE
   Interesting, exciting, and enjoyable work-*high*
   Good use of the skills and knowledge God has let me gain-*very high*

72

Personal growth and advancement within the company-*high*

Compensation in keeping with my contribution-*high*

Top management support of my efforts-*low*

Flexibility to be actively involved in church work-*very high*

The opportunity to help others live more fulfilling lives-*medium*

PRESERVE

The quality of our family life and relationship-*high*

My physical health-*high*

Personal integrity on the job-*very high*

A lifestyle that glorifies our Savior-*high*

AVOID

Interference with my participation in the church's activities-*very high*

Compromising my witness as a Christian-*very high*

Any situation where people do not seem committed to high quality in both product and service-*high*

This ranking of the criteria gives Doug a "feel" for the total range of relative importance among his criteria. It helps him to narrow down the number of criteria he has to compare to arrive at the most important criterion, or goal.

When he showed Sherry this measurement of his criteria to help him achieve his purpose with the decision he would make, she helped him get a little more specific. She asked, "What specific skills and knowledge do you want to put to use on any job you take?"

Doug thought for a minute, then said, "I am not a product man. My skill is in interpersonal relationships, in helping people achieve top levels of performance through guidance and motivation." As he was saying this he suddenly recognized that it was this that had initially attracted him to the New Hampshire opportunity.

Looking further down the list, Sherry asked, "What do you really want to preserve about our family life, about the relationships in our family? It had been some time since they had discussed this, and it was this point that particularly concerned her when she thought of the move. His new position could well take him away from the family more than his present one did.

"I like to be able to be home for supper most evenings. That's when we really open up to each other and share what has been happening to us. And I love to take off with the trailer for a weekend out in the wilds. There have been some really special times for us during those weekends," Doug responded thoughtfully.

"Will New Hampshire provide similar opportunities?" Sherry asked, recognizing that she already knew part of that answer.

As they continued to discuss the criteria they were joined by Jim. Doug explained what had been going on and let Jim look over the ranking he had done. Jim had hardly started reading when he turned to his father, "You know, that's what I like about your present job. You come home excited about it, telling us such interesting things about what goes on at the office. I hope I get a job some day that involves me in so many different things."

Doug knew that Jim was right. His present job did meet one of the key criteria for job satisfaction in his life. Amazing how complicated it could get! He realized that he'd have to do a fine-tuning on the ranking of the various criteria. Thus he set about revising his objectives, and the new set looked this way:

CRITERIA

a. Provide new, challenging, and varied tasks.

b. Permit sufficient time for preparation and attendance at church committee meetings, work projects, etc.

Doug moved this up because Sherry had reminded him how important his church participation had become, and how much satisfaction it had provided him. "You've really grown spiritually through the interaction with other spiritually-minded persons at church," Sherry had said.

c. Achieve personal growth and advancement within the company.

d. Good opportunity to put to use my skills in helping people achieve top levels of performance through guidance and motivation.

e. Maximize my earnings.
f. The opportunity to help others live more fulfilling lives.
g. Have sufficient opportunity to share evening meals and weekend outings with the family.
h. Preserve my physical health.
i. Avoid interference with my attendance at Sunday worship services.
j. Avoid any compromising of my honesty.
k. Only join a division with high quality performance standards.

As he looked over the criteria again, Doug realized that some of them were "musts" with him. Others were desirable but not absolutely essential. So he asked himself, "What are the requirements that any solution has to absolutely satisfy to be acceptable?" In other words, what requirements, if not met by any particular alternative, would cause him to immediately, without further questioning, reject that alternative?

Was this step really necessary? Is it important that you ask yourself this question?

Consider what happened at a large public utility. When the management of the utility decided to replace its fleet of service trucks used by linemen, they assigned a task force the selection of a model most suitable for the utility's purposes.

After an extensive, six-month analysis of requirements and examination of vehicles, the task force settled on a Volkswagon van. They prepared a detailed presentation with charts, diagrams, and other visual aids showing how the Volkswagon van best fit their needs. They even provided a fully modified van as an example of what could be done. Following the presentation the president commended the task force on their skill and persuasiveness in presenting their recommendation. Then he pointed out, "Unfortunately, you failed to take into account that as a publicly owned utility we cannot purchase a foreign vehicle."

What had gone wrong? The president had failed to pass along the one absolute requirement, that the vehicle be domestically manufactured. And the task force had not asked themselves, "What are the absolute requirements for this vehicle?"

You may consider an absolute criteria rather harsh because it eliminates some options that may otherwise be very attractive. In fact, they may be more attractive in all other ways than the alternative options. Yet that is exactly the function of the absolute, to protect you and ensure that you do not select an alternative that would violate beliefs, values, requirements, or absolute constraints.

That kind of situation faced the president of a major hotel chain several years ago. When the city ordinances of a major resort area were changed to permit the operation of gambling casinos, the board of the hotel chain saw it as a significant opportunity to make an entry into the casino business. The president, with clear Christian convictions about gambling, acknowledged that the board had the right to make a decision committing the corporation to a casino. Yet he also felt he needed to make a personal stand, so he informed the board that because he could not condone gambling he would submit his resignation if the board decided in favor of a casino operation.

The board ultimately decided that the opening of a casino hotel in that resort area was in the best interests of the corporation and its stockholders. The president, true to his absolute requirement stemming from his Christian convictions, resigned. He took the consequences gladly because he did not want to compromise his Christian testimony.

Earlier we indicated that you need to be specific and precise in establishing your criteria, the goals you want to achieve, the things you want to preserve and avoid. While this is important in establishing *desirable* requirements, those objectives that any decision *should*, rather than *must*, achieve, it is essential that absolute requirements be specific and measurable.

An absolute requirement is, by definition, unequivocally essential. Because of that any possible solution that fails to satisfy it should be eliminated from further consideration. This means that there should be no ambiguity or "stretching" of meanings.

The necessity to be specific may mean that the absolute requirement should be quantified. If a salary level, for example, is an absolute requirement to accepting a job offer, then the minimum salary level should be stated: "Salary level not less than $25,000 per year" rather than "an acceptable level of salary." Or if cost is a limiting factor in the purchase of a gift for someone, that upper limit should be stated: "Cost not to exceed $50," instead of "Not too expensive." The trick is to stick to it.

As Doug examined his criteria for the absolutes, he realized that most of them really did not quality as "musts." The one that came closest to being an absolute was "Avoid interference with my attendance at Sunday worship services" and "Avoid any compromising of my honesty."

"Do you know if the New Hampshire situation requires a lot of Sunday work?" Sherry asked him.

"They told me that the previous manager had worked only one Sunday when there was a fire in the plant," Doug said. "That's not really a violation of the absolute, for even Jesus said you'd get an ox out of the pit on Sunday."

Doug and Sherry concluded that compromising of honesty was more an ongoing situation rather than a specific condition at the New Hampshire plant. The plant was not involved in the manufacture of any product sold overseas that might require under-the-table money.

Having come to terms with the absolute requirements, Doug recognized that his earlier "rough cut" system of establishing priorities was not a fine enough tool. He needed to go to a system with finer shadings of significance.

At ExecuTrak we have found that using a numerical range from 0 to 10, giving the most important criteria a 10, is an effective way of doing this. Each of the other criteria will receive a numerical value based on how important it is *compared in ratio* to the one receiving a 10. For example, an objective regarded as only one-third as important as the one receiving 10 should be given a 3. And a 0 means it is less than one-tenth as important and not worth considering. Now you may like a different scale(say 0 to 20), and we leave it up to you to work with a system with which you feel comfortable.

Once Doug had settled on the 0 to 10 system, he enumerated his Decision Criteria.

To meet Doug's purpose the job *Absolutely must:*

a. Avoid interference with my attendance at Sunday worship services, except during emergencies.

b. Avoid any compromising of my honesty.

c. Provide a salary of $50,000 a year ("You should get a raise if you are being asked to take on a more challenging position," Sherry reminded him.).

Value   Desirable objectives:

10   d. Provide new, challenging, and varied tasks.

10   e. Permit sufficient time for preparation and attendance at church committee meetings, work projects.

9   f. Achieve personal growth and advancement within the company.

7   g. Good opportunity to put to use my skills in helping people achieve top levels of performance through guidance and motivation.

5   h. The opportunity to help others live more fulfilling lives.

9   i. Have sufficient opportunity to share evening meals and weekend outings with the family.

8   j. Preserve my physical health.

9   k. Only join a division with high quality performance standards.

Notice that Doug put his absolute requirements up front. That way he would not overlook any of them before evaluating the relative importance of other objectives.

Sometimes you will have absolute requirements that are also included in the list of desirable objectives. This may be done to give credit to options that do better than the absolute minimum results you require, yet cost less than the maximum resources you can spend in time, money, space, and so on.

Do not be concerned if you do not come up with any absolute requirements after you ask yourself, "Which one or more requirements, if *not* satisfied by an alternative, would cause you to immediately reject it from further consideration?" In some decision situations you may find that you have only desirable objectives. This could happen if there simply are no results that must be achieved above a minimum level—or if there are no ceilings on the amount of resources you have available.

You will probably find, as did Doug, that it is not easy to assign values to your desirable objectives, for this is not merely a numbers game. Your task is to try to establish the relative importance of each criteria. By assigning a 5 to "The opportunity to help others live more fulfilling lives" Doug is really saying that even though this criterion is important, it is only half as important as "Permit sufficient time for preparation and attendance at church committee meetings, work project."

Okay, you say, but I sure wouldn't weight the different criteria the way Doug did. That does not mean that Doug is wrong—or that you would be wrong. In your judgment, in the light of your experience and achievements, you may have different needs and values.

A most helpful question when trying to establish the relative value of each criterion is, "Is this criterion more, less or equally important as the criterion I have rated most important?" When you do this you will occasionally find yourself going back over the list and selecting a different criterion as the most important, upping its numerical value. Again you may find yourself giving several criteria the same numerical value because in your mind they actually are on the same level of relative importance. Even though they are quite different, Doug gave a 10 to both *d* and *e*.

Once you have finished the rating, you may want to double-check the accuracy of your judgments by comparing the less important ones against the higher-rated objectives. Is there still that much of a difference between them in your mind?

Of significance is that Doug rated his commitment to his church a full 10, or 15% (on top of his "absolute" on Sunday worship attendance), personal achievement objectives a total of 31 points, or 46%, family relationships a 9, or 13%, physical health an 8, or 12%, and quality products a 9, or 13%.

By categorizing such criteria, you can gain a better understanding of the proportionate effect of various factors in evaluating alternatives. Once you see the results you may even decide to go back and reassess and modify your list of criteria and/or their numerical values. In Doug's case his son Jim commented, "You sure don't seem to rate us very high, Dad, in comparison to achieving personal satisfaction." That hit Doug like a sledgehammer and resulted in some serious reassessment of priorities that evening. He became aware that imperceptively he had fallen prey to the "me first" syndrome so pervasive in secular society. And he thought he had really given God first place!

Step Four, setting priorities, thus helps you to differentiate absolute requirements from your desirable objectives, to put first things first and last things last. If possible, complete this step before you think of any possible alternatives (Step Five). Why? If you have a pet solution in mind you may inadvertently favor it by setting high values on the criteria it meets particularly well. That won't happen to you? Unfortunately we remain all too human, even when we think we have reached spiritual maturity.

For your test of the system before applying it to your particular decision, let's go back to the problem we presented with the Crisis Intervention Center. We asked you to think through what you would want to *achieve, preserve,* and *avoid* by any action taken because of the use of illicit drugs at the party. With those criteria in hand, review and critique the following list of criteria developed by the executive board of the agency. Consider which, in your judgment, would be absolute requirements, which would be desirable objectives, and what should be the relative importance of these desirable criteria through the weight you give each.

PURPOSE: Determine the best way to ensure the moral and professional integrity of the agency.

ACHIEVE
A. Mimimum disruption of agency services.
B. Future adherence to agency policies and regulations.
C. Fair and impartial treatment of the violators.

PRESERVE

D. Staff and board respect for the leadership of the executive director.

E. Commitment of the board members to serve on the board.

F. Agency's reputation for high-quality professional service to our clients and the community.

G. Attractiveness of the agency as a place of employment.

AVOID

H. Demoralizing staff and volunteers.

I. Loss of funding by government and community agencies.

J. Adversely affecting referrals from other agencies and the courts.

Once you have evaluated these criteria and assigned them numbers rating their relative importance to your way of thinking, you are ready to move on to Decision Building Step Five: Your search for solutions.

Chapter 7

What Are My Choices?

STEP FIVE

"Dad," Jim said as he looked over his father's paperwork, "I'm puzzled. Here you've got all these lists, even one with numbers beside everything, and yet you haven't even listed what you could *do*. Isn't what you are going to do the most important part of your decision?"

Jim's reaction to Doug and Sherry's process is not an unusual one. Most of us think that the most important thing to consider is what we can *do* about a problem requiring a decision. We feel safest if we have a list of alternatives, of options, in front of us. At least there's something we can *do* about it then. There's nothing as paralyzing as the feeling that there are no options!

Yet taking the short cut in decision-making by first listing the things we can do can make us overlook some truly creative alternatives. Remember what happened to the task force for the public utility company? Their process of determining that a Volkswagen van was the best alternative failed to establish the one absolute—no foreign vehicle. And it cost them plenty in wasted time and energy, as well as company money.

You could, of course, resort to that old question, "What did we do last time when I faced a similar decision?" Or maybe you are action-oriented and habitually ask yourself, "What's the quickest way of taking care of this?" You can by-pass all that time-consuming process of determining what you want to achieve, preserve, and avoid. Many a parent angry over a son or daughter's inexcusable behavior has jumped all over their teen, only to regret the alienation that resulted. This could have been avoided if they had asked themselves, "What do we want to achieve, preserve, and avoid?"

Though not quite as quick a fix, the selection of only two alternatives is all too common. On the surface this is more sophisticated, and it certainly is more open to the pros and con approach, but it again severely limits options. You know the kind of question, "Should I join this church or not? Should I teach Vacation Bible School this year or not? Do we insist that our 15-year-old attend evening services or not?" Maybe you ought to check out a few more churches. Or you possibly ought to be considering a summer teaching assignment in the Sunday school? And possibly mandatory attendance at a boring service in the evening is the "last straw" in a deteriorating relationship with your 15-year-old. Creative alternatives in each case will, however, surface only if you develop a clear statement of what you have to decide or determine.

Every summer churches across the country ask themselves, "Should we go back to the park for our Sunday school picnic?" What would happen if instead of answering simply yes or no, the Christian Education Board chairman were to ask, "What can we do that will mean the least dislocation after the morning service, yet provide a quick alternative if it rains?" One church decided on a barbecue next to the church, put someone in charge of games, and set up a loudspeaker for more effective communication. No lost families on the way to the park, no one worried about rain, no payment of park entrance fees. And everyone had a good time—and access to ample washroom facilities!

The use of criteria, as described in the previous chapter, in selecting alternatives can help you look beyond obvious choices. This process can help you design entirely new and innovative solutions. It can also help you combine or modify the best features of several alternatives in such a way that the combination really satisfies.

When Doug and Sherry first discussed the opportunity to move up the ladder by accepting the assignment in New Hampshire, they thought they had an either-or situation. Stay put and hope for an even better opportunity, or move across the country and hope it would work out. As they developed the criteria on what they wanted to achieve, preserve, and avoid, and then rated them according to their importance, Sherry suddenly said, "You know, Doug, maybe the move to New Hampshire isn't the only alternative to staying where you are. Maybe God let this opening come your way so you would think seriously about other opportunities. If we are seriously considering a move across the country, along with the uprooting effect this will have on the life of our children, maybe we should think of short-term service for the Lord. Like a couple of years on a service project in Africa or Indonesia. You are looking for new, challenging, and varied tasks, and I suspect a service project could provide those."

"You're right as usual, Sherry," Doug said. "But you know I won't get any $50,000 salary doing that."

"Okay, I think you deserve that in a corporate position, but I'm sure we can get by on much less serving the Lord in Nigeria, for example," Sherry countered.

"We'll have to talk to the kids, but let's put it down as an alternative to test against our criteria."

Doug knew what Jim might say, but the two girls could respond differently! Yet three alternatives certainly looked better on paper than two.

What Doug and Sherry experienced is duplicated many times—and sometimes by committees as well. Consider the case of a Midwestern interdenominational church in a suburban community with a dwindling youth program. The most recent youth sponsor had proved less than satisfactory and the Youth Committee had determined to look for a new one. A description of the position requirements had been sent to two theological seminaries and the placement office of a nearby college. Applicants had been narrowed to three persons. Before they tackled the review of the final three applicants, they re-read the job description they had provided months earlier.

"This will be a part-time position requiring the planning and conduct of bi-weekly meetings with young people of the church from September 1 to June 30 of each year. Activities will include Bible study, social events, and five weekend trips or retreats. The applicant must be a college or seminary graduate, preferably with a degree in teaching or the human services area. Salary offered is $1,200 per year, with a standard rate per mile to cover automobile expenses.''

The Youth committee consisted of Harrison Wilton, 61, a retired military officer and currently senior deacon of the church; Mabel Dawes, 55, a former school teacher; Philip Laird, 46, the pastor for the past five years; and Judy Merrivale, 27, a new member of the church. Bill Davis was chairman. In what seemed to Judy a clear move to establish an early favorite Bill began the discussion with, ''I think the first candidate we should discuss in Terri Sanforth. Harrison and Mabel know her well. She is the daughter of the former minister of our church and is currently working as a bank clerk while attending college in the evenings. She is 22 years old, majoring in human services, and needs just nine more academic credits to complete her degree requirements.''

Harrison quickly chimed in, ''I know that she does not yet have her degree, but she plans to have it by the end of the year. She's a good candidate, and I certainly think she ought to be considered.''

Judy sensed the drumbeat for Terri escalating when Mabel added, ''Terri certainly was very active in our church, assisting and teaching the junior high grades of our Sunday school and she is still singing in our choir. She has always been outspoken against the use of alcohol and drugs by teenagers, and is very respectful of adults. I think she sets an excellent example for our young people.'' A particularly heavy emphasis on ''excellent'' told Judy that Mabel certainly was ready for a positive vote in favor of Terri. She decided to play the devil's advocate anyway.

''What relevant experience has she had? You know she's hardly more than a kid herself.''

Mabel was ready for that one. ''Terri helped organize and supervise games and craft activities for the summer Bible school for several years. As part of her college fieldwork requirements she has worked with two social agencies and received supervision in administrative work and counseling. I realize she has not had much experience, but she is a very responsible person. Once she knows what she is expected to do, she is determined to accomplish it."

Judy realized the pastor would be no pushover when he said, "I knew Terri for about a year before she went to college. I certainly agree that her behavior is exemplary. However, I did overhear some comments from youngsters at summer Bible school that Terri is considered somewhat a snob and a 'cold fish'! We have already said that it is very important for a person in this position to relate well to these young people."

Harrison quickly responded, "That may be true, but I think you'll find most people agreeing that, once you get to know her, she can be very friendly. In her interviews with us she was certainly cordial, polite, and obviously interested in the position."

The silence after these comments was finally broken by Judy when she asked, "Haven't we said in all of our notifications that a college degree is required? Didn't we reiterate that earlier tonight?"

Finishing his notes, the chairman said, "Yes we did. But we should be practical about this too. It will be only a short time until Terri has her degree. I agree with Harrison that we ought to consider her a candidate for the position. If *you* knew her, you would see why."

The committee seemed stuck on Terri when the pastor suggested, "I attended a decision-making workshop at the church conference last month. I learned some things that might be helpful to us now in organizing our thinking and helping us come to an agreement. With your permission, let me show you the system I learned. Maybe it's worth a try."

Everyone nodded in agreement, so the pastor went to the front of the room, took a piece of chalk at the chalkboard and said, "We know we have a decision to make. We also know the problems with the last director that led to his dismissal, forcing us into this decision process. Our purpose for the decision, as I understand it, and you are free to disagree, is to *Determine the Best Candidate for the Position of Youth Program Director.*"

Sensing the agreement of the group he wrote it at the top of the chalkboard. Then he asked, "What are the things we want to achieve, preserve, and avoid by the decision we make?"

86

Mabel quickly answered, "One of the things we want to achieve is to have a director who can serve as a good example for our young people."

"Phil, I think you are right in pointing out that the person we hire should be able to relate effectively to this group of 13 to 16 year olds," said Bill Davis.

For a moment the group weighed the question. Then Mabel again chimed in, "This person should also be able to work well with the members of the Youth Program Committee. We certainly had our problems with the other one."

Amid general nodding of agreement Judy offered, "We need someone who is either a seminary graduate or has a college degree, plus experience."

The pastor turned from the chalkboard.

"We've mentioned the need for experience serveral times. But the word 'experience' is hard to get a handle on. We may not all be talking about the same thing. Experience in doing what?"

Harrison responded, "Good point, pastor. One of the things that a person has to be able to do is to carry out the program directives with a minimum of supervision."

"And another," said Bill, "is skill in planning and supervising recreational activities."

"Don't you think the ability to communicate the gospel of Jesus Christ and lead Bible studies is important as well?" asked the pastor.

By the time everyone had added what he felt needed to be achieved, preserved, and avoided, the chalkboard looked like this:

PURPOSE OF DECISION
Determine the best candidate for our position of youth program director.

CRITERIA
Serve as a good example for our young people.
Can relate effectively to age groups 13 to 16.
Seminary or college graduate.
Be able to work well with members of the Youth Program Committee.

Able to communicate the gospel of Jesus Christ and lead
Bible studies.
Be able to carry out program objectives with a minimum
amount of supervision.
Skill in planning and supervising recreational activities.
Be able to provide counseling and guidance to young people
having personal problems.
Have knowledge of community resources where young peo-
ple can find additional help,

A pleasant coffeebreak later the committee reassembled for
further refining of their selection process. The pastor began with
the question, "Which criteria are so important that no candidate
is acceptable unless he or she meets all of them?"

Judy, the stickler for meeting the educational requirement,
plunged in.

"I guess we have to resolve whether or not we're going to
insist that our candidate must have graduated from seminary
or college. In the way you phrased the question, if we say it's
an *absolute* necessity that the person be a graduate, we can't
even consider Terri Sanforth."

"Bill, what do you think?" the pastor asked.

After a moment of reflection Bill responded, "Now that I've
thought more carefully about it I certainly would not want to
rule out the candidacy of a good person if he or she has only
a few more credits to complete. However, I don't think we
should consider having more than a regular semester's work
to complete for graduation, which I believe is 15 credits. It
seems to me that if a person is in his or her last semester, they
are pretty strongly motivated to finish up their work and get
it over with. I do think we are all agreed that such a level of
training is an important qualification, a necessity."

All of the committee members agreed with Bill's point. Thus
the previously discussed absolute requirement of having a college or seminary degree was revised.

"Are there any other requirements that any decision absolutely has to satisfy in order to be satisfactory?" asked the pastor.

"I really feel strongly that the person we select should attend worship services regularly," said Harrison.

"I agree that this is very important," rejoined the pastor, "but how will we be able to measure that? I mean, what do *you* mean by regular? After all, there may be totally acceptable reasons for a person's not attending worship services every single Sunday."

"Seems to me," said Harrison, "that this is important enough to be an absolute requirement. We can leave it to the pastor to assess whether the individual is regular in attendance or not, since he will be closer to the situation."

General agreement resulted in this requirement being listed as an absolute condition for employment.

"Okay, now that we have established what we want to achieve, preserve, and avoid, and what the absolute requirements are for every director, we can assign values to each of the criteria to indicate their importance relative to one another," said the pastor.

After taking a rough cut at the criteria in terms of high, medium, and low importance, the pastor asked the group, "Among the criteria we have graded high in importance, which is the most important, second most important?"

Mabel readily replied, " 'Serve as a good example for our young people' is most important, I think."

Bill Davis revealed his concern. "Seems to me that being able to communicate the truth of the gospel is critical for kids at that age."

When no other single criteria was promoted as most important, the pastor asked, "Would being able to communicate the truth of the gospel be equally, more, or less important than that the person we select be a good example for our young people?"

"I think being a good model is most important, since at that age they tend to copy the people they like. Anyway, we all learn more from what other people are than from what they say."

Everyone agreed with that, quickly moving on to a 10-point scale suggested by the pastor. They gave the criterion "serve as a good example for our young people" a 10. The pastor then asked, "If this criterion receives a 10, what value should we assign to 'Able to communicate the gospel of Jesus Christ and lead Bible studies'?"

By concensus this criterion was assigned a 9.

At this point the pastor reminded the group that they already established as absolute requirements "within no more than one semester of fulfilling graduation requirements" and "acknowledged by pastor to be attending no fewer than 70% of Sunday worship services, a percentage that the pastor had decided represented 'regular attendance'. " Since these are minimum requirements, they may wish to give more credit to candidates who exceed these mimimums—and "doing better than the mimimum" thus should be included among "desirable objectives."

As the group examined the absolutes they had set up they agreed that the first one was sufficient. Yet they also felt that it would be desirable for the best candidate to exceed the 70 per cent attendance requirement. After more discussion the attendance requirement was listed with the "desirable objectives" as well and given a 4 rating. After that they were able to assign values to the remainder of the criteria.

DESIRABLE OBJECTIVES

10 Serve as a good example for our young people.
9 Be able to communicate the gospel of Jesus Christ and lead Bible studies.
8 Can relate effectively to age group 13 to 16.
7 Skilled in planning and supervising recreational activities.
7 Able to carry out program objectives with minimum amount of supervision.
6 Able to provide counseling and guidance to young people having personal problems.
6 Able to work well with members of the Youth Program Committee.
4 Faithful church attendance.
3 Knowledge of community resources where young people can find additional help.

"Let's now list the candidates," said the pastor. "We have Terri Sanforth. She certainly seems to meet our absolute requirements. Whom else should we consider?"

Picking up an application from the table, Bill Davis said, "We have Ron Gleason, 26 years of age. He graduated from seminary two and a half years ago, was assistant minister for a year with an interdenominational church in a nearby community, and left this post to take a position with a youth rehabilitation agency in the same community. He is now coordinator of their youth outdoor skills program. Ron is responsible to a large extent for developing that program and supervising the teenagers in it, all of whom are street kids and some of whom are drug abusers. The program was designed to get the kids off the street and build confidence in their capabilities through experiences in hiking, camping, rock climbing, and canoeing. Ron also serves as manager/player on a community softball team. He has given his agency notice of his resignation to attend graduate school, where he will be majoring in pastoral counseling."

"Well, he certainly meets the educational requirements," said the pastor. "We'll have to ask the minister of the church he is now attending to see if he attends church regularly. Who else should we consider?"

"The other candidate," said Harrison, "is Joseph Harkness. He is 28 and a social studies teacher at the high school in town. He lives in Stanton(a small town approximately nine miles away), where he and his wife Mary are active in their church. They both sing in the choir, and he is chairman of the finance committee and teaches Sunday school. In addition to his church work, Joe serves on the board of directors of a local social agency serving the elderly. I do not think he will have any trouble satisfying either of our absolute requirements."

Pastor Laird listed all three on the chalkboard. As he did so Mabel turned to the others.

"I think we may be overlooking another option. We have mentioned several times that the candidate should meet certain experience requirements. And we have mentioned some of the specific skills that experience should include. There is, however, a youth service advisor now on the staff of the executive council of our church who periodically holds workshops and programs in planning, supervising, and youth counseling. I understand that he is also available to individual churches to give instruction and assist youth directors in these various areas of activity. Suppose a person did have deficiencies in any of these areas. Couldn't we use him as a consultant to any one of the candidates?"

"That is an excellent idea, Mabel," said the pastor. "So in addition to the three candidates by themselves, we have each of them possibly assisted by the consultant."

We hope that by now our "walking" you through examples has given you enough experience to feel comfortable with this approach. How good you feel about using this approach will determine if, how, and how well you will use these techniques."

What insights have we shared in this chapter?

Foremost is to let your criteria generate your alternatives, not vice versa. Only after the pastor put the committee through the "achieve/preserve/avoid" exercise did the members set aside their pet candidates and begin seeking common ground.

Important also is the fact that you do not need to be bound by obvious or stated choices. Your criteria could prove helpful in discovering other, often better alternatives. Mabel, by using the "experience" criteria as a springboard, was able to come up with another set of options.

You can greatly improve the possibility of having this happen if you stop at each criterion and ask, "What are the possible ways of achieving, preserving, or avoiding this one?" And persist in asking, "What ELSE can be done?" Explore all options, even the ones that may seem questionable at first. Most err on the side of too few, not too many alternatives. Don't forget that you can combine the strengths of possible solutions for even better new alternatives.

Great, you are saying, but all of the examples presented are really quite positive, with pleasant options. Does this process really work when you are involved in an unpleasant decision-making situation?

Remember the Crisis Intervention Center? The executive committee was faced with, "How do we make the best of a bad situation?" Some members clearly felt helpless, convinced it was a hopeless mess. When this is the case a group can become apathetic and easily distracted from the decision they need to make. Consequently it is even more important to have some process, some mechanism, that can keep the group from getting bogged down, that will enable members to see clear progress toward a solution.

The results of the executive committee's deliberations regarding the purpose, criteria, and possible solutions to this difficult problem appear in the chart. Though it is fairly clear from the chart what was done, an explanation of some of the elements may prove helpful.

PURPOSE: Determine how best to ensure the moral and professional integrity of the Agency.

CRITERIA	Alternative A Retention of program director- Dismissal of other 4 violators	Alternative B Dismissal of all five	Alternative C Two months suspension of pay for program director- Dismissal of others	Alternative D No dismissals - written warnings in personnel files
ABSOLUTE REQUIREMENTS NO loss of ANY client referral source	Yes	Yes	Yes	No
DESIRABLE OBJECTIVES Value				
10 Preserve reputation for high quality professional service to clients and the community.				
10 Avoid loss of funding by government and community agencies.				
9 Future staff adherence to agency policies.				
8 Fair and impartial treatment of the violators.				
8 Minimize disruption of agency services.				
7 Staff/board respect for executive director's leadership.				
6 Avoid demoralizing staff and volunteers.				

The Executive Committee established as an absolute require-ment, "*No* loss of *any* client referral source." Though many peo-ple come to the agency for help on their own, referrals from other social agencies, churches, schools, and the courts are a *key* source of clients for the agency, particularly in the area of adolescent and drug counseling. The loss of any one of these sources could prove disastrous to the reputation of the agency and its ability to meet the needs of the community.

Also, funds necessary to support the programs and salaried staff of the agency have to be applied for each year. Funding agencies typically conduct annual reviews of the agency's per-formance. Those evaluations, plus a detailed proposal and budget, are used by the funding agency to determine if their contract with the agency will be continued. These considera-tions were the basis for assigning values of "10" to the first two Desirable Objectives. The search for solutions resulted in the four Alternatives that you see listed across the top of the chart.

There was much reluctance among members of the commit-tee to terminate the employment of the program director. He *had* done an outstanding job, was well liked by the members of the staff, and he had "only taken one puff," criticized himself and the group for smoking marijuana, and left the building. One member suggested to the committee that they, too, played a role in the violation by allowing alcoholic beverages to be brought onto the premises in the first place (as it was a com-munity and not a church function). "Therefore," he argued, "there shouldn't be any dismissals, but rather formal warnings should be administered to prevent any further occurrence" (Alternative D).

You may be wondering why the analysis of this decision so far has been set up in the particular form appearing in the chart. The next task in the decision process is to compare the alter-natives to determine which *best* satisfies our criteria. We have found that the matrix form you see here is the most convenient layout for making such comparisons.

One other feature about the matrix needs explaining. In the column under Alternative D, you see a large X. This is our way of signifying that an alternative has been rejected as soon as it fails to satisfy even one absolute requirement. "No dismissals, with written warnings for each of the violators" was rejected as an alternative because it *would* undoubtedly result in the loss of referral sources. Though some other social agencies tend to be more lenient regarding such violations (because of the problems that you can run into with a volunteer work force), the courts, schools, and very likely churches who referred people to the agency for help would probably stop referrals if they found out that the agency had not taken direct, punitive action against agency members guilty of smoking marijuana. Given that fact, Alternative D was dropped from any further consideration and would no longer be part of the analysis.

In the next chapter, you will discover which of the remaining alternatives were selected as we discuss step six: Test Your Alternatives.

Chapter 8

Which Choice Is Best?

STEP SIX

The idea of several years on a Third World Christian service assignment intrigued Doug. Since the idea had come from Sherry, he knew she would give it a fair chance against the other alternatives. After mulling it over for several days, and again discussing it with Sherry, he introduced the idea at supper with all three children present.

"You all know I've been offered a new position in New Hampshire. Mom and I have been discussing it, trying to determine not only the effect on me but also on you. The other day Mom suggested we consider a Christian service assignment in another country like Nigeria, Indonesia, or one of the South American countries. Before we go any farther I'd like to hear what you think of it."

Forty-five minutes later Doug and Sherry had a rather good idea how their children felt about such a move. As a result Doug got on the phone to the denominational headquarters the next day. He discovered that a new agricultural college was being established in Nigeria and an experienced administrator was needed as business manager. He asked that all pertinent information be sent to him, including information on educational opportunities for the children. Then he called the Nigerian consulate and talked with the information officer.

"Sherry," he said that evening, "in a few days we'll have the kind of information we need to make Christian service a third alternative."

Remember Doug's depression from the first chapter? What has happened to transform him from a person paralyzed by fear into a confident, moving-ahead person? Yes, Sherry's support is a key factor, but more important is the decision-making process that got him off dead-center.

Earlier we mentioned committee discussions that seem to go round and round without ever getting to a decision-making point. More often than not the reason is disagreement over the alternatives, with dominant personalities each pushing their option. They need an objective standard to *test the alternatives*. This is Step Six in the decision-making process.

Sure, you say, but isn't that why we developed the criteria, what we want to achieve, preserve, and avoid?

Right, because once you have those clearly defined you can go on to evaluating each possible solution against every criterion. The alternatives that successfully pass through your screen of absolute requirements must next be evaluated against each of the desirable objectives. To do this objectively, however, you need information on how each alternative performs on the criterion you are using to measure it.

Doug's action after Sherry suggested a third alternative illustrates a key principle in all of this: *The quality of any decision can only be as good as the quality of the information on which it is based.*

"I don't have the time for that," you say.

Doug's method reveals that information-gathering need not be as time-consuming as it may initially appear. Modern communication systems can give us vast amounts of information quickly. In fact, the sheer volume of information can be counter-productive.

Remember your last visit to an automobile salesroom? A fast-talking salesman had your head spinning with facts and figures on the car he was selling. You were soon reeling with what is called "information overload."

Your decision criteria can help avoid both of these dangers. By keeping what you want to achieve, preserve, and avoid in mind, you can limit your information-gathering to your criteria—how that alternative does against each criteria. Your criteria also help tell you what is important for you to know about any alternative, so you do not waste time and effort gathering information that will ultimately prove unimportant or even irrelevant.

Another way to avoid information overload is to make your information "visible" by writing it down. Some authorities on brain functioning say that we cannot think about more than seven bits of information simultaneously. Even if your decision has as few as six to eight objectives, and three or four alternatives, you have a minimum of eighteen separate bits of information to keep in mind as you evaluate the alternatives. With that overload it is easy for some of the facts to get lost.

Finally, remember our discussion on how the inability to justify our decision to others can paralyze the whole decision-making process? You can eliminate that paralyzing fear by writing down the critical information that led to your decision, making it easily accessible when someone questions the validity of your conclusions.

In this chapter we will "walk" you through three examples of evaluating alternatives against the criteria. The first is the selection of the youth director, the second is Doug and Sherry's situation, and the third is the Crisis Intervention Center. We will chart the evaluation process and provide some understanding of the process.

"Now that we have established the purpose of our decision-making process, set up the criteria for what we want to achieve, preserve, and avoid, determined what our absolute and desirable criteria are, we can list the six possible alternatives on the chalkboard and evaluate them against the criteria," said the pastor, Phil Laird. He drew six columns on the chalkboard, listing the alternatives on top and the criteria down the left side.

"Everyone ready?" asked the pastor. "Lets start with 'serve as a good example for our young people'. What do we know about Terri that indicates she would be a good example?"

"Well," said Mabel Dawes, "we know she sings in the church choir, has taught Sunday school, and is an outspoken critic of the use of drugs and alcohol."

The pastor began writing down the information while commenting, "Yet remember that she has some problems in communicating Christ's love. Members of her Sunday school class did not perceive her as a caring person."

Discussion revealed that other members also considered this important, so it was added to the list.

"How about Ronald Gleason. What sort of example does he provide for our young people?"

Judy responded, "He is a seminary graduate and works in a youth rehabilitation agency, both of which are to be respected."

"Yes," Bill Davis said, "but I certainly would not show up for an interview in blue jeans, polo shirt, and sneakers. His hair is long even by teenage standards. I find him much too casual in appearance and behavior."

"I couldn't believe his language," said Mabel. "I was really offended by his frequent use of four letter words during our interview."

"Look," said Judy, "he was not really cursing. He obviously felt pretty strongly about some things. If you'll recall, his earthy language occurred when he was talking about the lack of understanding that many adults have about young people and their reasons for stealing and using drugs."

"Judy," said the pastor. "I can understand where you are coming from, but there is no way I am going to have an assistant who cannot express himself strongly in everyday English and has to resort to four-letter words. Seems to me that his language alone should disqualify him."

"I wouldn't go as far as that," said Harrison. "Let's leave him as an alternative and see how he rates on the other criteria. After all, we cannot lose much simply considering him."

"Okay, but he clearly does not set a good example, and I want that noted," said Mabel.

The others quickly agreed and the pastor noted the comments in capsule form on the chart. Harrison Wilton then began the discussion of Joseph Harkness.

"I've learned from his pastor that Joe is very active in church, as is his wife. He teaches Sunday school and is chairman of the finance committee. He is obviously devoted to his wife and six-year-old son."

"Anything else on how he might set an example to our young people?"

The silence led to the next question, "How might a consultant help each of these people become a better example?"

"I suppose a consultant might help Ron improve somewhat. Yet I have learned from people who attend the church he served that complaints about his casualness and his language did not bring about improvement. I do not think a consultant could be of much help to Terri and Joe."

Everyone agreed, and they moved on to the next objective.

"What do we know about Terri's ability to communicate the gospel and lead Bible studies?" the pastor asked.

"Every report I have heard from her Sunday school teaching has been positive," said Mabel. "Her involvement in vacation Bible school also shows her concern for communicating the gospel."

"And Ron?"

"Even though he is a graduate of a seminary recognized for having sound Bible teaching, he does not seem to be concerned about that. I have a feeling he is in reaction to something in his background," said Bill.

"Yes, but he did work with young people in another church," said Judy, whose own preference was beginning to show.

"Since we do not have any positive information let's put down only what we know," said the pastor. "I'm convinced, however, that this is a danger signal."

"And Joe?"

Harrison plunged in: "He is both a teacher in public school and a Sunday school teacher at church. He is thoroughly involved in the ministry of the church, and I am sure could do a good job in Bible study classes with the young people."

Since there were no dissident voices, the pastor entered this on the chart.

"Would any of these be helped by a consultant?" the pastor asked.

"I could see Terri responding to some instruction on how to make the gospel on Jesus Christ relevant to the teen today, since she has been working largely with children," said Bill. "Seems to me Ron's orientation is to social, recreational and community involvement. Since he has not been open to helpful suggestions in the past, I doubt a consultant could change his attitudes. And Joe really does not need help, according to my reports."

The pastor noted those comments after checking on any possible disagreement among the committee.

This sampling of conversation during the preparation of the chart indicates the dynamics of the process. Now examine the chart itself for the rest of the conclusions reached for each alternative.

PURPOSE OF DECISION: Select the best candidate to fill the youth program director position.

Criteria	Alternative A Terri Sanforth	Alternative B Ronald Gleason	Alternative C Joseph Harkness
Absolute Requirements			
Minimum of 15 credits to fulfill remaining graduation requirements.	Yes - 9 credits remaining	Yes - Graduated	Yes - Graduated
Acknowledged by minister to be regularly attending services (at least 70% of Sunday services).	Yes	Yes	Yes
Desirable Objectives			
Serve as a good example for our young people.	+ Sings in the church choir. + Has taught Sunday school + Very outspoken against the use of drugs and alcohol. − Not seen as a "caring" person.	+ Seminary graduate. + Works in Youth Rehabilitation Agency. − Uses profanity. − Dresses inappropriately. Too casual.	+ *Very* active in church. + Teaches Sunday school. + Chairman of finance committee. + Devoted family man.
Can relate effectively to age group 13-16.	− Described as "cold fish," and as a "snob" by young people. In mixed age groups, − tends to associate with older adults rather than people her age.	+ Outstanding rapport. Very accepting of them and they of him. + Reported as being a "neat guy", "cool."	+ A junior high school Social Studies teacher. Very well liked by his students. + They report really enjoying his classes, which they say are very interesting and that they learn a lot.

Criteria	Alternative D Terri Sanforth with Consultant Assistant	Alternative E Ronald Gleason with Consultant Assistant	Alternative F Joseph Harkness with Consultant Assistant
Absolute Requirements			
Minimum of 15 credits to fulfill remaining graduation requirements.	Yes	Yes	Yes
Acknowledged by minister to be regularly attending services (at least 70% of Sunday services).	Yes	Yes	Yes
Desirable Objectives			
Serve as a good example for our young people.	Same as A (+ + + −)	Might improve with some counseling by consultant. However, prior complaints did not bring about improvement.	Same as C (+ + +)
Can relate effectively to age group 13-16.	Consultant could provide a limited amount of help.+	Same as B (+ +)	Same as C (+ + +)

Desirable Objectives	Alternative A Terri Sanforth	Alternative B Ronald Gleason	Alternative C Joseph Harkness
Able to communicate the gospel and teach Bible studies	+ Has taught Sunday school and summer Bible school	– No information on teaching + Is seminary graduate + Communicates to teens	+ Experienced teacher + Sunday school teacher + Active in church
Skilled in planning and supervising recreational activities.	+ Helping organize and supervise games and craft activities for elementary grades of vacation Bible school for 2 successive years. – No employment experience in recreation.	+ Developed, coordinated and supervised youth outdoor skills program (i.e., hiking, camping, rock climbing, canoeing). + Manager and player on community softball team.	+ Services on curriculum planning committee of the school. + Much experience with family camping and hiking. – No employment experience in recreation.
Able to carry out program objectives with minimum amount of supervision.	– Generally lacking in experience. + Determined to succeed and sometimes fails to recognize the need for help soon enough.	+ Successfully administers and conducts agency program with only occasional review by executive director.	– Would need more committee supervision than (B) particularly in the beginning, but not as much as + (A) or for as long.
Able to provide counseling and guidance to young people having personal problems.	+ Took 1 semester course in interviewing and counseling techniques.	+ Received seminary and agency training in counseling. Frequently has to counsel troubled youngsters in his program. + Has their trust and confidence.	+ Students sometimes come to him to discuss personal problems. Known among students as "a guy you can talk to who cares and tries to help you." – No formal training in counseling.

Desirable Objectives	Alternative D Terri Sanforth with Consultant Assistance	Alternative E Ronald Gleason with Consultant Assistance	Alternative F Joseph Harkness with Consultant Assistance
Skilled in reinforcing religious values with social service orientation.	Consultant will help her improve discussion techniques. (+)	Same as B (+ +)	Same as C (+ + +)
Skilled in planning and supervising recreational activities.	Consultant could help significantly in planning programs, not as much as in supervision. (+ −)	Same as B (+ +)	Has good basic planning and supervisory skills for consultant to build on. (+ + −)
Able to carry out program objectives with minimum amount of supervision.	Could not make as effective use of consultant as (C). (−)	Same as B (+)	Would recognize where consultant can be most helpful, and make good use of him. (+)
Able to provide counseling and guidance to young people having personal problems.	Lack of *any* counseling experience would limit amount of help consultant would provide. (−)	Same as B (+ + +)	Would benefit from counseling work and consultant assistance. (+)

	Alternative A Terri Sanforth	Alternative B Ronald Gleason	Alternative C Joseph Harkness
Desirable Objectives			
Able to work well with members of Youth Program Committee.	+ Personally admired and respected by committee members who have known her since childhood. + Follows orders very well.	− Casualness of dress and manner of speaking offensive to committee members. − Does not respond well to criticism.	+ Very confident of his abilities; cooperative with those whose ability and knowledge he respects. + Continually wants to know reasons behind directions from those whose ability he questions.
Faithful church attendance	+ "Excellent - rarely misses a worship service."	+ "Good - averages approximately 3 services per month."	+ "Excellent - tries very hard to meet with his Sunday school classes *every* Sunday and then attends worship services.
Knowledge of community resources where young people can find additional help.	+ Is knowledgeable about youth services, particularly in this area.	+ Has personal contact with a member of youth services organizations. Knows how they work. − Not familiar with services within this particular area.	− Limited familiarity with youth services.

Desirable Objectives	Alternative D Terri Sanforth with Consultant Assistance	Alternative E Ronald Gleason with Consultant Assistance	Alternative F Joseph Harkness with Consultant Assistance
Able to work well with members of Youth Program Committee.	Same as A (+ +)	Same as B (— — —)	Same as C (+ + +)
Faithful church attendance.	Same as A (+)	Same as B (+)	Same as C (+)
Knowledge of community resources where young people can find additional help.	Same as A (+)	Same as B (+ —)	Consultant could advise him in terms of what to look for and how agencies typically work. (+)

Now that you have read through the chart imagine yourself in the shoes of Pastor Laird, Bill, Mable, Harrison, or Judy. How would the development of this chart affect your confidence in reaching a good decision? Obviously the chart does not yet give you any final answers. That's why you now need to move into the final step of testing the alternatives, since you can now measure the worth of each alternative against the criteria for what you want to achieve, preserve and avoid. That final step is scoring all the alternatives on a one to ten scale to see which best satisfies each criteria, then totaling the points for any over-all status.

To do this relatively easily we suggest a three-step testing process:

1. First, using the best information you can gather about each alternative, rate each option against each criterion, using the same principle you used with the criteria. In other words, the alternative that does the best job of satisfying that particular criterion rates a 10 (even if it does not do a perfect job). An alternative that does only half as well by comparison with the highest-rated alternative only gets a 5, and so on, *in ratio* to the other.

2. Second, once you have completed step one for all alternatives against each of the criteria, multiply the *value* of each *criterion* by each *rating* you have given to each *alternative*. This will provide you with a score for each of the options which takes into account the relative importance of the criterion against which the option is being rated.

3. Third, add the total for each alternative against all the criteria to determine which alternative over-all does the best job, which second best, etc.

Let's illustrate this process with the Youth Program Committee selection process. We tune in as the pastor is saying, "Now that we have gathered and recorded the most important information about each alternative, we are ready to determine which of our options is the best solution. Beginning with our first desirable objective, which of our alternatives does the best job of achieving that particular criterion?"

The group agrees that, based on the information they have considered, alternative C (Joseph Harkness) should provide the best example for the young people among all of the candidates, with or without the help of a consultant.

"Okay, let's give that alternative a 10," said the pastor. "Now compared to Joe, how well do we feel that Terri Sanforth satisfies that criterion?"

"That's tough," said Harrison. "Both are very active in church and both teach Sunday school. Terri is closer to their age and that may be more impressive to young people than someone older when he makes the same kind of statements. It is very close. I think we ought to rate Terri a 9."

"Yet we must remember that she is rated as not a very caring person," said Bill. "Joe, on the other had, has much love for his family. I have the feeling that this quality is important to kids, and I would rate her at best a 7 or 8."

After discussion the group settled on 8 as best representing Terri's relative contribution to achieving the first objective.

"I assume that we are now ready to talk about Ronald Gleason," said Mabel. "He should not get more than a 1 as far as I am concerned."

"That's not right," interjected Judy quickly. "You are judging him strictly on the language you heard. You must remember that he has been a most successful role model in working with kids who have been on drugs and alcohol."

"True," said the pastor. "Except for his language and appearance he communicates many qualities we would like our young people to have."

"I would settle for a 3," said Harrison.

A 3 he became, as the group moved to considering what the additon of a consultant might do to affect the ratings.

"Clearly the addition of a consultant would not add to either Joe's or Terri's ability to be a good example, so alternative D or F would be rated the same as A and C. However, we felt that Ron Gleason might improve some with counseling by the consultant who, as a fellow professional, he is likely to respect. So how should we rate this option?"

Bill replied, "On the chart we see that past complaints have really not brought about much improvement. Given that information, I do not think we should rate that option more than a 4."

Note that the pastor's instructions and questions regarding the ratings to be assigned each alternative continually emphasize that the ratings should be based on the best information they have. In addition, the options were to be rated according to how well they compare to the "best" alternative achieving that criterion, "Serve as a good example for our young people."

After rating all of the alternatives for each of the criteria, the ratings of each alternative are then multiplied by the values assigned to the corresponding criteria.

On the completed chart that follows, the respective ratings for each alternative against each of the criteria appear in the column headed R (Rating) under each alternative.

You may find it helpful to see how what was said in the group session was recorded on the chart and applied in the computations. The scores resulting from multiplying the alternative rating by the criterion value appear in the columns headed R x V. The last of the three steps, testing the alternatives, is to add up the individual scores for each alternative. Those total points also appear on the chart below, indicating that the "winner" is Joseph Harkness *with* consultant assistance (Alternative F, with 554 total points).

The following chart provides an abstract of only the ratings and calculations from the *Desirable Objectives* section of the chart. Transfer these ratings and totals to the earlier chart to get the "big picture."

ALTERNATIVES

CRITERIA

CRITERIA	A R	A RxV	B R	B RxV	C R	C RxV	D R	D RxV	E R	E RxV	F R	F RxV
10 Good Example	8	80	3	30	10	100	8	80	4	40	10	100
9 Teach Bible	8	72	5	45	10	90	9	81	6	54	10	90
9 Relate Well	4	36	10	90	10	90	5	45	10	90	10	90
7 Planning	3	21	10	70	6	42	5	35	10	70	9	63
7 Program	4	28	10	70	5		5	35	10	70	9	63
6 Counseling	4	24	10	60	7	42	5	30	10	60	9	54
6 Work with YPC	10	60	3	18	6	36	10	60	3	18	6	36
4 Church Atten.	10	40	8	32	10	40	10	40	8	32	10	40
3 Community Resources	10	30	8	24	4	12	10	30	8	24	6	18
		391		439		452		436		458		554

When you combine these numerical values with the earlier chart listing the strengths and weaknesses of the alternative candidates, you have a rather clear roadmap of the decision process. You can also see what information was used, why it was used (it referred to specific criteria), and how the information was applied in choosing the best alternative. The chart is also most useful in explaining to others how you reached your decision. Even if others have contradictory information or disagree significantly with your judgments you have a basis for a more intelligent discussion.

Yet how large a difference in total points is necessary for you to feel confident that one alternative is actually superior? Consider the difference between the candidates for youth director. Joseph Harkness, without benefit of consultant assistance (alternative C), had 498 points for the second highest total. Third highest was Ronald Gleason with consultant assistance (alternative E).

When the selection committee saw this the pastor commented, "You can now see how important it is to have absolutes that screen out really quite good alternatives with a fatal flaw. Language unacceptable to a Christian should have been an absolute that disqualified Ronald Gleason before we took all that time considering him."

Suppose, however, that Ronald Gleason had not disqualified himself with his language. Is the point difference between him and Joe Harkness enough to make Joe a clearly superior choice? In our experience a difference of 15 percent is normally adequate, if this alternative also scores well on *each* of the highly-rated desirable objectives. If your choice meets both these tests you can be reasonably confident that it is indeed the best solution.

Going back to our example, we can subtract 15 percent from 554 and we get 470, which puts Ronald Gleason right on the borderline at 458 (with consultant assistance). Yet in this case he also scored low on one of the high-ranking objectives, "Able to communicate the gospel of Jesus Christ and teach Bible studies." And even though C is lower than E, it is close enough to F minus 15 percent to make Joe Harkness a clear choice.

But what if two or more of the possible solutions are indeed close? Then consider first what your emotions tell you—which alternative feels the best. If there is one alternative that you intuitively feel is better, ask yourself why you feel that way. Is it the Holy Spirit guiding you, or were you not quite on track during the charting process? The following questions could be helpful:

1. Did you state your purpose correctly?
2. Are there additional things to be achieved, preserved, or avoided that you failed to state as criteria (remember the problem with Ron's appearance and language)?
3. Do the values you assigned to the criteria accurately reflect your priorities?
4. Have you overlooked any other alternatives that deserve consideration?
5. Are you confident of the accuracy and completeness of the data you used to rate your alternatives, especially the heavily weighted criteria?
6. Did you use a 10 rating for the alternative that best satisfied each criterion, and ranked the others in ratio accordingly?
7. Did you make any errors in arithmetic?
8. By looking at where the existing weak points are in each of the strong alternatives, can you combine particular strengths of each to fashion a truly superior solution?

You will remember from some of the conversation on the committee that even in assigning numbers we are guided both by our subjective values and specific objective facts. Judy felt more emotional about Ron and was harder on Terri, for example, while Mabel had quite different feelings about Ron and Terri. The best decisions reflect both knowledge and values/feelings, and also take into account the feelings of those people who should be involved in and/or will be affected by the decisions.

Though Doug and Sherry had developed strong emotional ties to family and friends through living a long time in one place, the decision-making process helped them focus more clearly on the alternatives. They were forced to assume a level of objectivity they would never have achieved simply by writing down pros and cons. Let's look over their shoulder at the completed chart, which had acquired a fair number of erasures as the whole family worked on it.

"I'm amazed at the amount of self-evaluation we've gone through in this charting," concluded Doug. "We probably should go through this exercise every few years!"

As you look over the chart remember that if your family were to go through the charting process it might have quite different scores. Each family values some things higher than other families. This is particularly true if there are children at home or older parents to care for.

PURPOSE: Determine the best way to apply the talents God has given me.

CRITERIA ABSOLUTE REQUIREMENTS	KEEP JOB (A)			NEW HAMPSHIRE (B)			NIGERIA (C)		
Avoid Sunday worship interference.	Yes			Yes			Yes		
Avoid compromising honesty.	Yes			Yes			Yes		
Provide $50,000 a year*	Not immediately			Yes			No		
DESIRABLE OBJECTIVES		R	RxV		R	RxV		R	RxV
Value									
10 Provide new, challenging, and varied tasks	+ Jim is right - this is a strength	10	100	+ Should be most interesting because I will be general manager.	10	100	+ Every indication is positive	10	100
10 Permit preparation for and attendance at church committee meetings, work projects.	+ Can generally be done	8	80	− Will be very difficult because of learning new role.	4	40	+ Could well be a positive factor	10	100

* Later reconsidered and judged as probably not an absolute requirement.

CRITERIA

Value	KEEP JOB (A)		NEW HAMPSHIRE (B)		NIGERIA (C)	
	R	RxV	R	RxV	R	RxV
9 Achieve personal growth and advancement within the company.	− Have largely reached my limit — 4	40	+ Great potential — 10	90	− None	
7 Opportunity to help people achieve through guidance and motivation	+ Some opportunities / − Limited by a more task-oriented job. — 5	35	+ Most attractive feature. — 10	70	+ Excellent opportunities — 10	70
5 The opportunity to help others live more fulfilling lives.	− Not on the job / + Through my church and community work. — 3	15	+ Both on the job and in the community — 10	50	+ Great opportunities — 10	50
9 Share evening meals and weekend outings with family	+ Is now possible — 10	90	+ Close enough to go home even if working overtime. — 9	81	− Family will have to be split up for part of the year. — 5	45
8 Preserve my physical health	+ No problems — 10	80	− New and heavy role could be physically taxing. — 7	56	− Totally new culture could endanger health — 5	40
9 Join division with high quality performance standards	+ Definitely the case — 10	90	− Needs a lot of help — 4	36	− Start from scratch — 4	36
		530		523		441

"You know, Sherry, you may think it strange," said Doug after looking over the results of their charting, "but I have realized as we were doing the charting that the discipling process, the pouring of myself into others, has become very important to me. At this point I could care less about a big salary, about advancement within the company. Remember what Jesus said, 'Except a corn of wheat fall into the ground and die, it abideth alone: but if it die, it bringeth forth much fruit.' "

"What you're saying," Sherry said, "is that the Nigeria experience is like planting wheat."

"Right. We would spend our lives for people whose life is almost spent already because they need help to improve their food production," said Doug. "I wonder if with these new insights we should not set up a new purpose and new criteria and go through the whole process again. I suspect the totals would come out differently."

Doug's and Sherry's experience illustrates the significance of charting alternatives in trying to come to terms with our real inner commitments. The discipline of the process is the catalyst God can use to help us gain new insights.

Finally, let's move to that emotion-laden decision-making process at the Crisis Intervention Center. Members of the board felt strongly about their positions and were ready to fight for them. The executive-director recognized the potential for major explosions, but he also saw how the ExecuTrak decision-making process could channel those strong feelings into more objective expressions.

The one area of agreement was that very soon the public would be aware of the marijuana-smoking incident. For this reason it was too big and important an issue to go unheeded. Take time as you study the chart to get a good picture of the cross-currents running through this decision-making. Refer to the chart as we explain some of what went on in the analysis and dicussion.

PURPOSE: How best to ensure the moral and professional integrity of the agency

Criteria	Alternative A	Alternative B	Alternative C	Alternative D
Absolute Requirements No loss of *any* client referral source.	Retention of program director and dismissal of other four violators. Yes - There should be no loss.	Dismissal of all five. Yes - No loss	Two months suspension of pay for program director. Dismissal of others. Yes - No loss	No dismissals. Formal warnings. Will lose 2 or 3 referral sources.
Desirable Objectives **Value**				
10 Preserve reputation for high quality professional service to clients and the community.	Program director has proven experience and ability to effectively develop and administer youth foster care programs, but involvement in drug use could be disastrous to *his* reputation and the agency's. 3 30	An indication to the community and clients of the importance the agency attaches to the moral and professional behavior of its staff. Less competent assistant would have to temporarily take over. 10 100	Less competent assistant would have to be acting program director temporarily, but suspension plus dismissal of others more likely would be seen as a way of preventing re-occurrence. 5 50	
10 Avoid loss of funding by government and community agencies.	Such a compromise would be resented by funding agencies, future financial support probably would be reduced for the Foster Care Program. 4 40	Indicates to funding agencies our refusal to tolerate *any* violations of the moral integrity of the Crisis Intervention Center. 10 100	Funding agencies would consider this more acceptable than (A); not as good as (B). 6 60	
9 Future staff adherence to agency policies.	Would breed attitude that if you're in management, you can get away with breaking the rules. 5 45	Position of agency on such violations unmistakably clear, but doesn't totally eliminate the possibility of future violations. 10 90	Indicates a lower degree of acceptance of such violations than (A). 8 72	

PURPOSE: How best to ensure the moral and professional integrity of the agency

CRITERIA

Desirable Objectives Value	Alternative A		Alternative B		Alternative C		Alternative D
8 Fair and impartial treatment of the violators.	Program director clearly given preferential treatment because of past performance and supervisory status. Past efforts of others not acknowledged.	5 40	All violators treated as equal. All know and understand policy and had heard the executive director's warning.	10 80	Still display partiality to program director, but not as much as (A).	7 56	
8 Minimize disruption of agency services.	Program planning and implementation minimally affected.	10 80	Loss of program director would significantly lengthen time it will take before Youth Foster Care Program becomes *fully* operational.	2 16	Implementation will be delayed, but not as much as with (B).	5 40	
7 Staff Board respect for executive-director's leadership.	Inconsistent—His policies say one thing; his actions something else. His personal friendship with program director may be seen as deceiving factor. Supervisor should be setting a *good* example.	3 21	Shows that he stands firmly behind his policies and directions, and can make difficult decisions.	10 70	Not as firm on his own policies and regulations as (B). Friendship may still be seen as coloring the final choice.	6 42	

Absolute Requirements Desirable Objectives Value	Alternative A	Alternative B	Alternative C	Alternative D
6 Avoid demoralizing staff and volunteers.	Program director has been particularly well liked by members of the staff, but they also resent his "stupid" behavior and what it could do to the agency. 8 48	Some staff members state that dismissal of program director or would be *too harsh* because his involvement was "minimal." Agree that others should be "fired." 5 30	Staff members feel that some punishment of program director is appropriate. 10 60	
6 Maintain board member's commitment to continue to serve on the board.	One threatens to resign if program director is not "fired immediately" along with the others: "What the program director did was wrong!" 7 42	Commitment would be strengthened according to four board members. 10 60	Same as (A). 7 42	
4 Maintain attractiveness of the agency as an employer.	A reputation for tolerating staff drug use would act as deterrent to desirable candidates. 5 20	Minimizes adverse effect on agency reputation. 10 40	Agency would be seen as only slightly less tolerant of staff drug use than (A). 6 24	
2 Minimize administrative problems.	Required executive-director supervision of Youth Foster Care Program remains about the same. 10 20	High involvement of executive-director until replacement found for program director. 3 6	Executive-director supervision of Youth Foster Care Program increased. 5 10	
TOTAL POINTS:	(383)	(592) **THE WINNER**	(456)	

Two points became clear quickly when board members were asked to share their reaction to the first criterion as it related to each alternative. First, the program director had been doing a very professional job. Clearly, he would be difficult to replace. Secondly, his involvement with drugs, however slight, would seriously hurt his reputation as a professional. Because of this anything less than his dismissal, together with that of the other four people, would also seriously hurt the agency's reputation for high quality professional service. From the chart you can see that the alternatives are thus more heavily weighted in the direction of the expected moral reaction of the public.

Now you may have noticed the somewhat higher scores given the first criterion over against those for the second criterion. Funding agencies tend to be less severe in their indictments of this behavior because of their more frequent involvements with such incidents. They also have real reluctance to lose highly qualified staff. The funding agencies would be less likely to punish the entire agency by withdrawing funds from other programs, with the exception of the one funding the Foster Care Program.

Now look at the information and ratings of each alternative against the criteria, "Future staff adherence to agency policies." Even though the dismissal of all five violators may do much less than a perfect job of eliminating the possibility of future violations, it does the best job of the three alternatives. Therefore it gets a 10. The other alternatives are then rated in ralation to this alternative and its high rating.

Look also at the sixth criterion, "Staff/Board respect for executive-director's leadership." According to the agency's by-laws, the final decision on personnel matters rests with the executive-director. He could, if he chose, ignore the decision reached through this group's deliberations. Therefore his acceptance or rejection of the alternatives can be judged independently of the judgments made by members of the board.

Emotional exchanges characterized the discussions on "Avoid demoralizing staff and volunteers" and "Maintain board members commitment to continue to serve on the board." The program director of the Youth Foster Care Program was very well liked, and even affectionately regarded, by several of the staff members and volunteers. Despite their resentment at his "stupid" action, they remained loyal to him. Yet one member of the board threatened to resign if all five persons were not dismissed. He struck paydirt with, "People, what is right is right. What is wrong is wrong. His violation is not a matter of degree. What he did was wrong!" Though some members may have been less morally offended, or chose to remain loyal to the agency despite their differences, they all agreed that their commitment would be strengthened if the executive-director were to dismiss all five.

In the light of this you may wonder at the relatively low value of 6 assigned to each of these two objectives. Once again, however, we are evaluating their importance relative to the most important criteria. In this case the highest weighted objectives relate to the actual survival of the agency.

Based on the facts and collective feelings of the group, the best tentative solution thus is alternative B, the dismissal of all five violators. This conclusion became inescapable despite the personal friendship between the Foster Care Program director and the executive-director. What was not mentioned was that the program director was also a former student and close friend of the chairman of the board. The sadness and frustration complicated the picture, but the process made the group's selection of the best alternative unequivocal.

You may have noticed the use of the word "tentative" when applied to the solution growing out of STEP SIX: Test the alternatives. In the next chapter we discuss the final step, learning how to anticipate and cope with the problems and changes in the environment that could weaken and undermine whatever you decide should be the best tentative solution.

Chapter 9

How Do I Get Decision Insurance?

STEP SEVEN

"You know, Doug," Sherry said several days after going through Step Six, the charting process, with her husband, "I keep having a funny feeling that something is going to go wrong if we go to Nigeria."

That's Sherry, Doug thought as he held out his cup for another cup of coffee after a delicious supper. *Always looking at the dark underside of everything.* Although he could get "down" before making a decision he moved forward decisively once a decision had been made. You simply had to have faith, faith in God and faith in the ability He had given you to meet every difficulty.

"There you go again," he chided Sherry. "Even if the sky is blue you're sure to find a cloud in it. I believe we can trust God to be with us even in the difficulties of life, once we are clear that we are in His will."

Sherry knew Doug was right, but something told her that the caution she felt should not be ignored. Maybe it was just her super-caution she felt should not be ignored. Maybe it was just her super-cautious nature, but maybe it was also the Holy Spirit.

"I know it's hard to think of what might go wrong. Yet I think we ought to be realistic. After all, Jesus warned us to 'count the cost.' Isn't that what you call a tough look at the future?", Sherry suggested.

"Okay, I'm game to seeing what could go wrong. Some days you just make too much sense," he said with a smile as he again searched through a nearby drawer for a piece of paper. "If we are going to do this thing right, we might as well get everything down on paper."

As Doug and Sherry embark on what we call Step Seven, "Trouble-shooting your decision," let's consider why some people simply refuse to take this step. One reason is that when people have invested their time, effort, and best thinking into reaching a decision they find it difficult to imagine that anything could seriously go wrong. And the more experienced you are in decision-making, the more likely you are to overlook the significance of Step Seven. This is especially true if you have several clear indicators of God's guidance, the kind of coming together of "coincidences" that seem to shout, "You made the right decision."

Charles Blair in his book, *The Man Who Could Do No Wrong*, took this attitude after his decision to build a Life Center in Denver. He had just toured the site after two clear "confirmations" that the vision for a geriatric center was of God. Surely his reluctant wife would now agree.

"When that night, in the seclusion of our bedroom, I related the day's experiences, she once again failed to catch the vision. . . . 'It seems to me, Charles, that you're already stretched to the breaking point. Where will you find time to listen to God when you're already working 26 hours a day?'

"It was like a bucket of cold water thrown on the fire of my excitement, and I came up sputtering. 'How long do you have to listen, when the need's in front of your nose?' "

Seventeen years later, after the nightmare of cost over-runs, delays, fund-raising difficulties, and conviction of fraud by a jury of his peers, Charles Blair wrote, "The protection a husband and wife provide each other can be extended (or supplied, for the unmarried) by entering into relationship with a small group of men and women committed to lift one another regularly to the Throne of Grace. Such a group provides not only support but—crucial in any time of building—correction."

Trouble-shooting your decision is one way of providing correction before you get too far along. Simply asking yourslf, and those involed with you in the decision process, "What can go wrong?" can make a world of difference. This discovery came belatedly to a junior choir director preparing for the special Christmas program. Five weeks before the program she selected her soloist and was heavily involved in rehearsals with him when she discovered, with three rehearsals to go, that the soloist would be out of town that weekend. After a painful session with a very disappointed boy, she had to quickly find a replacement. If she had only asked "What could go wrong?" she might have checked with the children's parents on who would be out of town. Or she surely would have prepared a stand-in, just in case the star soloist took ill.

Or consider the decisions made in connection with the grand opening of a research center for a truck manufacturer. To highlight the end result of the research, the planners arranged for a new diesel truck to be moved into the inner court of the center. Great care was taken to make sure the truck's exhaust stack would not touch ceilings as it passed through the building to the inner court. Yet when at 8 a.m. of the great day the truck moved into the building, disaster struck. The hot gases from the exhaust stack set off the sprinkler heads in the ceiling, spraying water over a large area of the room.

Unfortunately, the maintenance person who knew where the cut-off valve was located was at home enjoying his Saturday off. By the time he was contacted there had been a lot of water damage . . . and the whole celebration had to be called off. Now if only someone had asked, "What can go wrong when a truck emitting hot exhaust gases passes through our shiny new rooms?"

Recently one of the authors decided to replace the worn, outdated heating system in his home. During his investigation of heating systems he checked into different kinds of automatic stack controls. These are designed to close off the flow of hot air into the chimney after the furnace shuts off. During one of these dicussions with a heating systems salesman he asked, "Well, what happens if the stack control doesn't open the chimney when the burner goes on again?"

After some stammering, the salesman lamely said, "Of course, we warn our customers about the danger when we recommend this device." He had no good answer for, "What could go wrong?" That in the light of the fact that the furnace could explode if the shut-off valve did not open!

How then can we prevent our decisions and actions from getting derailed or undermined by such problems? There are three basic steps involved in *Trouble-Shooting Your Decision*:

1. What could go wrong with the tentative solution you have chosen? List all possible problems that come to mind.

2. Roughly calculate the *likelihood* of each of the possible problems occurring and their respective *impact* if they do happen.

3. Determine what actions should *prevent* those problems that have a high likelihood of occurring. Consider the serious impact if they did occur, and what actions should *minimize* their consequences if they still occur.

At the Youth Program Committee meeting to select a program director we see these steps illustrated.

"Okay, we have now decided that Joseph Harkness, assisted by a consultant, is the best tentative candidate," Pastor Laird said, stepping back to the chalkboard. "Yet at the church conference we were told about a final, most important step. We need to troubleshoot the alternative that we have determined achieves our decision criteria before reaching a final decision. The question we need to answer is, 'What could go wrong with it?' "

After explaining why we find it so difficult to even consider what could go wrong because of our emotional involvement with the decision, the pastor pointed to the question he had written on the chalkboard: "What could go wrong if we were to have Joe Harkness as our youth program director, with help from a consultant?"

Bill Davis was ready.

"He may resent having to work with, or even being advised to work with, a consultant."

"Good," said Pastor Laird as he wrote the comment on the board. "What else could go wrong?"

"I could see that the youngsters who have him as teacher in school may be reluctant to also spend evenings and weekends with him," said Mabel Dawes.

Judy Merrivale said, "Parents may object to his not being a member of *this* church."

"Another possible problem," responded the pastor as he wrote away at the chalkboard, "is that we want him to be a good example for our young people. Yet they may not be aware of his involvement in his own church. Is there anything else that could go wrong?"

"His other church and community responsibilities may interfere with his fulfilling his youth program obligations," replied Judy.

"And since we had the problem in the past," observed Harrison Wilton, "he may not keep the committee adequately informed of his program activites."

A long silence indicated that everyone had touched on his key concerns, so the pastor asked, "Could anything that might be disastrous happen?"

"Well," said Bill after another pause. "He may not stay on the job very long. If that happened we would lose the benefit provided by the consultant, plus the time and effort spent hiring and training him."

Another silence indicated that the members were ready to move on.

"Good work," said the pastor. "That's quite a list of potential difficulties. Now, since it is getting late, let's make best use of our time to concentrate on those problems that seem most critical.

"A way we can measure how critical they are is to use our general experience, and what we know about this particular situation, to determine how *likely* it is that any of these difficulties will occur, and what the *impact* would be if they did happen. What we found easy to do at the church conference was to evaluate each item of concern by first asking what would be the consequence of it happening in terms of high, medium, or low impact. Then, if it would be serious, we considered what would be the likelihood of it occurring: high, medium, or low.

"First question. What is the consequence of Joe resenting having to work with a consultant?"

"Well, Pastor," replied Bill, "I think it is important that we have the best thinking of the leadership of our church in this area, through the advice of the consultant. Yet it is true that Joe may just disregard what this consultant has to say. If this occurs, all of our effort and expense will have been useless."

"What impact would this have on the success of our decision, Bill, if it did occur: high, medium, or low?" asked the pastor.

"High, without a doubt," said Bill.

The rest agree, and the pastor wrote H under impact.

"What's the chance that this will happen?"

After a thoughtful pause, Harrison replied, "Pastor, we will be telling Joe right away that we are going to be providing him with the help of a consultant. As a professional, he should appreciate that. However, he has a lot of experience with young people, with program development and planning. So I would say that chances are medium that he will not use the consultant."

Again there was agreement.

"How strong an impact would it be if the young people he teaches at school are reluctant to spend evenings and weekends with him?"

"We're talking about so few children, Pastor Laird, that I think it would have low impact," said Judy. "Others may feel differently."

A quick sweep of the group indicated no disagreement, so L went up under impact. And because the impact of the problem occurring is low, the committee did not discuss the chance of it occurring.

"How serious is it that our young people may not know about Joe's involvement in his own church?" asked the pastor.

Bill responded, "I think it would have low impact. The example he sets when he is with them is far more important."

Since no further discussion was needed Pastor Laird asked, "What would be the consequences of parents objecting to Joe's not being a member of our church?"

"I can see why parents would prefer that he be a member of this church, but how serious is that?" asked Judy. I do not think they are going to keep their children from participating in the program if he isn't. I would say that it would have medium impact, at most."

"I disagree, Judy. I think it is more serious than that," said

Bill. "We count on the parents for a lot of help. We ask them to loan us camping equipment, provide transportation, and even chaperone at times. It is important that parents get a chance to see Joe frequently, and get to know him, if they are to volunteer their assistance, or even respond to requests for help. Because we have to rely on parents' support and direct assistance so much, I think the impact is high."

Mabel and Harrison quickly agreed.

"I wasn't aware that the program depends so heavily on the help of parents," Judy conceded. "That being the case, I have to agree that the impact would be high."

H is duly recorded on the board. Because of this pastor asked, "What chance is there that these things will happen?"

The committee agreed that the likelihood was High as well.

The possibility of Joe's other church and community responsibilities interfering with fulfilling his youth program obligations is rated, after some discussion, High in impact, but of Low likelihood. His failure to keep the committee adquately informed on his program activites is seen as having Medium impact on the overall program, with a Medium chance of occurring.

Pastor then asked, "What would be the consequences of Joe's not staying on the job very long?"

"If he were to leave, it would certainly disrupt the youth program again," said Bill. We would lose out on our investment in him, and much of the help provided by the consultant. So I think it should be rated High."

"How likely is it that this will happen, Bill?" asked the pastor.

"Well, he seems interested enough in the job, but because he is a very capable person, some other interesting and more challenging opportunity may come along for him. I think there is a Medium chance of this happening."

The Troubleshooting list looked like this:

WHAT COULD GO WRONG?

IMPACT	CHANCE	
H	M	May resent having to work with consultant.
L		The youngsters who are his students at school may be reluctant to also spend evenings and weekends with him.

L		Church youth may not be aware of Joe's involvement in his own church.
H	H	Parents may object to his not being a member of this church.
H	L	His other church and community responsibilities may interfere with fulfilling his youth program obligations.
M	M	May not keep committee adequately informed on his program activities.
H	M	He may not stay on the job very long.

Pastor Laird, smiling broadly, said to the group, "You know, you have really been doing splendidly. I hope you are as pleased with our progress on this decision as I am. With the work we have just done, we have been able to identify some possible problems that could be quite serious and that unfortunately have some chance of occurring. These are the most important pitfalls we need to be aware of. Now how do we prevent them from happening, or a least control them? Are there ways to minimize their impact if they do happen?

"We are particularly concerned that parents may object to Joe's not being a member of this church. This is the only one we rated High in impact and on chance. What can we do to prevent this concern from happening and possibly blocking Joe's effectiveness if he takes the position?"

You could almost see the wheels turning. Harrison finally said, "Obviously, we could ask Joe to join our church, or at least attend regularly. But I do not think that's right. After all, Joe's minister has shared information about him with us. Besides, we should not be raiding sister churches for members. What I think we should do is to get a letter out to parents of our young people explaining Joe's background and explaining what he is doing in his own church, and how important he has been and is to his church."

"That's a good idea, Harrison" said Mabel, "and maybe we could do that by having a special meeting with the children and their parents to introduce Joe to them and include what you have said in that introduction. He is a very personable young man, and this would give the parents a chance to meet and chat with him, get to know him better, and ask any questions that they may have. What do you think?"

"That is an even better idea, Mabel," replied Harrison, and the other committee members nodded approvingly.

"Suppose, as you suggested, Pastor," said Bill Davis, "that this does not work, and some of the people we have counted on in the past for help back out? What then?"

"I think what we would do in that case, Bill," answered the pastor, "is to visit these people personally, pointing out how important their help has been, and express our hopes that we can count on them in the future."

The pastor waited for other comments, then asked, "Any other suggestions?"

When he saw that no one had anything to add, the pastor continued, "Though we said that there is only a Medium likelihood that Joe may not stay on the job very long, the feeling was that it would be serious if he didn't. Should we try to think of ways to prevent this type of failure?"

Everyone agreed that it would be important to prevent this happening, yet no one seemed ready with a suggestion.

"Our conference leader who helped us learn this process suggested that when we are unable to think of possible ways to prevent problems, we try to think of reasons or causes for that problem occurring," said the pastor. "This makes it easier to come up with some solutions. Why would Joe want to leave?"

"One possibility that I can think of," said Judy, "is that he could become concerned about the amount of time he has to spend away from his family."

"That's quite possible," said the pastor. "Any suggestions on how to prevent this?"

Harrison answered, "We can suggest that he include his wife and child on some of the outings on which he takes the young people."

"Yes, we could" agreed Bill. "And another reason he may want to leave is that, after he has been on the job a while, he may feel that he is not getting paid enough. I guess one of the things we could do to prevent this is to tell him we will be reviewing his salary at the end of the year. If his performance warrants it, we will, if at all possible, increase his salary."

"But what if he does leave, despite all our efforts, after being with us only a year? How can we minimize the impact of this on the youth program?" asked the minister.

Bill answered, "I guess we just go through this same process again, maybe this time with the consultant, who might help us find some candidates. . . . "

The dialog you have just read illustrates how the troubleshooting process works in an actual, practical situation. Now you may have been asking yourself, "Why do you need to do troubleshooting of your decision when you already considered what you want to *avoid* in establishing the decision criteria?"

When developing the criteria it is best not to think of specific solutions, or you risk building the criteria to either fit or "shoot down" that possible range of solutions. So the types of problems you think about when you ask yourself, "What do I want to avoid?" really are developed to refer to *any* solution you may select.

When, however, you reach a tentative solution, this choice very likely will have its own distinctive characteristics, with one or more possible difficulties unique or distinctive to it. You would have a rather different set of problems with Ron Gleason from those listed for Joseph Harkness. Therefore, troubleshooting your tentative solution is an important step in safeguarding your decision.

At many conferences we have referred to the development of troubleshooting skills as "The Art of Negative Thinking." Troubleshooting is not to find reasons for avoiding making a decision and taking action, but instead to significantly increase the probability of success of the decision by the action you take.

There may be occasions when your probing for possible problems may turn up one, or even more, pitfalls or roadblocks that would have disastrous consequences not previously anticipated. And you may not be able to find any way to prevent them or initiate corrective action.

Some time ago, for example, a Federal Aviation Agency official reviewed plans for modifying a municipal airport. He turned up six separate problems that, he believed, were absolutely certain to occur, any one of which would make the airport inoperable. In a letter to one of the authors he reported that the planned changes in runways would make it impossible to properly coordinate several takeoff, approach, and landing patterns. Though these plans had been reviewed by several city planning board members and engineers, all had failed to identify even one of these problems. The best explanation he could offer for this failure was that the plans simply had not been examined with the question in mind, "What could go wrong?"

The airport modifications would have cost several millions of dollars. With the new information on the problems, the plans were sent back to the drawing board. It is clearly better to have an alternative "shot down" before any action is taken, rather than after it.

When Doug and Sherry sat down to troubleshoot their tentative alternative, they were joined by Jim. Doug wrote at the top of the sheet of paper, "What could go wrong?"

"Well, Mom has been having some problems with allergies," said Jim. "If we go to Nigeria she may discover that she is allergic to something that could have serious consequences."

"True," said Sherry, "but I would not rate the impact of that very high. If I can control my allergies here, I am sure those new ones can be controlled as well."

"Right," said Doug, "especially since we will be in close contact with a medical center. Seems to me that we could have a big problem with Trudy. She is not outgoing like you and Linda, and she does not have a natural group to join like Linda, our band member. How do we rate the potential impact of her developing personality or learning problems?"

"I'd rate the impact high both on her and us," said Sherry.

"What are the chances of this really happening?"

"I think there's a pretty good chance of it happening," said Jim.

"So we have two Highs, right?" asked Doug, They agreed. "What can we do to reduce the chances?"

"It seems to me that instead of sending her off to a boarding school I should work with her for at least a year. That way she can get acclimated to the enviroment and make friends of girls in our community. That should get us well started at least," said Sherry.

"I'd really like to finish my senior year of high school before you go to Nigeria," Jim finally said. "I hate being a wet blanket, but the British school system used in Nigeria is so different I would probably have difficulty graduating."

"What impact level do we rate Jim's problem?" asked Doug. Jim smiled.

"I'd rate it high, and the chances of it happening high as well."

"That means we may have to postpone our participation in the agricultural college for a year. If we did that they might have found someone else and not need me," said Doug. "Before we get too deeply into that, let's pray about it and see if we can think of any creative alternatives."

Doug put the sheet of paper with the rest of the papers worked up during the past week of decision-making. He recognized that as a Christian family they had to think through the impact of a decision on other members of the family. Troubleshooting the alternative is one way of doing it. Many of the most serious blunders that could have been prevented have occurred in decisions and actions affecting or involving loved ones.

Which brings us to the decision to discharge all five persons involved in the marijuana-smoking incident at the Crisis Intervention Center. The reactions of people, and the effects of the decision on them, can be seen from the list of possible problems developed during troubleshooting the decision.

IMPACT	CHANCE	WHAT COULD GO WRONG?
H	H	The courts and police officials may still be reluctant to make referrals to the agency despite dismissals.
H	H	We may have under-estimated the adverse reaction of the funding agencies, resulting in loss of funds.
H	M	Neighbors who have complained about youth offenders being counseled at an agency in their neighborhood may intensify their complaints against the agency's presence in their neighborhood.

H	M	Agency management and staff morale may be damaged by lowered public trust and confidence.
M	H	It may be difficult to get a qualified replacement for the program director.
M	M	Those persons discharged may be seriously handicapped in getting other jobs.
M	M	The public may still discredit the agency despite the dismissal of the offenders.
M	M	Local newspapers may be unwilling to carry agency advertisements and may withdraw their editorial support.
M	L	Some members of the board may feel guilty about the action and later say they do not support the decision.
L	M	Those persons discharged may speak disparagingly about the agency in public.
H	L	The dismissal of the two volunteers could leave the telephone shifts uncovered.
L	H	The decision may be appealed to the executive committee of the board of directors, particularly by the program director.

As you can see, that is a rather impressive list of difficulties developed, in spite of the careful analysis made of the complex emotion-laden issue. However, it was believed from the beginning that, regardless of the severity of the action taken against the violators, the damage done to the agency's reputation by their participation in using marijuana could be very serious, if not irreparable. The point to remember is that when you cannot completely correct any problem by a decision you make, it is even more important to troubleshoot your solution to prevent or minimize what could go wrong. Now on the other hand if you are not limited in what you can do to correct a situation, the discovery of many serious and likely problems would suggest that your decision may not be the best. You would do well to start your analysis all over again from the beginning, in that case.

How did the Crisis Intervention Center respond to the problems raised during the troubleshooting session?

In anticipation of the high likelihood of the courts being reluctant to make referrals despite the dismissal of all five, and in view of the fact that many of the agency's programs depended on referrals from the police and courts (particularly the Drug Rehabilitation Counseling Program and the Foster Care Program), it was decided to make full disclosure to the courts of what happened, what action was taken, why it was taken, and how it was taken. And the courts and funding agencies proved to be most understanding and supportive of the decision. Nor were there apparent adverse reactions from the neighbors or the public at large.

Replacing the program director did prove difficult. However, the preventive action of bringing the Foster Care Program under closer supervision of the executive-director, and providing additional training to the assistant to the program director, worked out quite well. Nor were there any serious delays in the program becoming fully operational.

Eighteen months later key people in the community, as well as the people within the agency, still felt very good about the decision to dismiss all five people involved in the marijuana incident.

As expected, the program director did appeal the decision to the executive committee. During the appeal the program director presented his case against the decision to the five members of the board of directors and a staff representative. After hearing from the program director and briefly deliberating, the committee unanimosuly rejected the appeal, supporting the executive-director's decision to dismiss him and the four other violators.

The chairman agreed to communicate the decision to the program director, even though the latter was a close friend and former student of the chairman.

"I wish your violation were such that I could simply boot you in the rear-end and let it go at that, but that is not possible," began the chairman. "The decision reached by me personally, and by every single member of the committee, is to uphold the decision of the executive-director to dismiss you, along with the four other people. I in no way regret this decision, because I think it is the best decision we can make. But I want you to know that I do deeply regret having to make it. What you did was absolutely wrong and inexcusable. By your actions, you seriously jeopardized the reputation and integrity of this agency. You knowingly violated the policy of the agency, and ignored the expressed warning of the executive-director against any such behavior. As a supervisor, you should have stopped what you saw was going on immediately. Instead, you participated in it. You have worked very hard, and have made significant contributions to this agency, so it is most unfortunate that these have to come to an end. . . . Is there anything you'd like to say?"

"No, you have been very clear," the program director replied and walked out, closing the door behind him.

Throughout the proceedings, the chairman's values had found expression in the defined *purpose* for the decision, the *criteria* and *values* assigned to them, the *alternatives* generated, their *evaluation*, the *troubleshooting* of the tentative solution, and the *final decision*. Though saddened by the entire situation, he felt completely confident that the decision had been right. The long term results proved it.

How would you describe the net result of this decision-making process? We think it is best expressed as follows: "The best decision is a balanced decision; one which logically best achieves the satisfaction of your criteria, including your feelings and values, and reduces your risks to an acceptable level." If you have been submissive to the leading of the Holy Spirit throughout the process, consistently seeking His guidance through prayer, you will find this a truly helpful process.

Section III

INVOLVING AND HELPING OTHERS IN DECISION-MAKING

Chapter 10

Should I Involve Others?

Is there ever a time when you should involve others in your decision-making? Is the Holy Spirit not enough of a resource for the Christian? When does involving others become a cop-out? If I involve others, won't they try to manipulate me?

As you read these questions you probably remembered situations where you involved others and wished you hadn't. Or you thought of situations where you had depended on people for answers and overlooked the need for God's guidance. Possibly you remembered hearing, "You and you alone are responsible for the direction your life takes. Don't ever let anyone take away that freedom."

As we discuss involving others in decison-making you will get answers to many of these questions and reasons why people hesitate to involve others. You will begin to see some of the benefits, as well as at what stage you can profitably let others share in the decision-making process. The examples will isolate situations where involving others proved benefical. At the same time these illustrations will model ways in which you can profitably involve others.

Probably the most important reason for letting others be part of the decision you are making is that they provide an added level of information, experience and perspective. Let's join Doug and Sherry.

"You know, Doug, I have a feeling that somewhere we are missing something," Sherry said as she cleared the table a couple of evenings later. "We did the best we could with the information we were able to gather—and you really did a good job on that, Doug."

Doug stretched his legs as he turned sideways at the table.

"Maybe so. I wonder if going over our seven steps with our pastor wouldn't be useful. He has counseled so many during a time when they have been considering a job change," he said.

"At Bible study today I heard that a missionary from Nigeria is going to be at a missionary conference near here. He could certainly help us understand what we could be getting into if we go to Nigeria," Sherry said as she turned on the water at the sink. "I realize that the decision is ours to make, but I would feel a lot more comfortable if they gave us their perspective."

Doug got up and headed for the telephone.

"There's no time like the present," he said, "and I'll never have more time than right now."

As in Doug and Sherry's situation, the broader information base of another person can be most useful. If your decison involves specialized knowledge, be willing to involve a specialist. Many a former small businessman, for example, would still be in business if he had involved a marketing specialist in decisions regarding strategy.

You may say, "I don't need that kind of help. But I need real teamwork if the decisions I make are to be carried out successfully." Nowhere is this more apparent than in the family.

One of the authors some years ago decided to finally take that dream trip across the United States. In the process the family ultimately went through parts of twenty-two states and the northern tip of Mexico, traveling 11,200 miles. At that point the family consisted of two girls, eight and fourteen, and two boys, seventeen and nineteen. The trick was to provide something for everyone.

From the beginning of the planning each member of the family participated in one way or another in every major decision. We quickly realized that relying on hotels and motels for lodging and meals would make the cost prohibitive. So we all attended a camping show, evaluating a wide range of recreational vehicles. We decided on a tent trailer that would sleep six comfortably and contained a stove, refrigerator, and a table for eating inside.

Supper frequently got everyone involved as we established the purpose, set up criteria, determined alternatives and tentative solutions. We took the time to troubleshoot our decisions, ultimately reaching decisions on final choices. Once it was all over we realized we had almost as much fun doing this as we had on the trip!

The seven-and-a-half week trip proved an overwhelming success, despite the fact that six people lived together in a station wagon and a tent trailer the whole time. The usual bickering among the children failed to develop, and everyone had a good time. All grew in their loving and caring for each other, even Mom and Dad. We are convinced that the most significant ingredient in the mix contributing to success was the teamwork developed during the decision-making process.

This kind of teamwork is also important in industry, especially when the decision to be made may have unpleasant consequences. At such a time the involvement of key personnel can actually prevent the sabotaging of the decision.

Some time ago we were asked by a division vice-president to serve as decision counselors for his management group as they faced a complex and ultimately unpleasant decision. Although the division was still making a good profit, the market for its product was shrinking fast. In addition, the corporation continued to use the division as its major "cash cow," draining its income to fund other, more promising, divisions. And because of the dwindling demand for the division's product, the corporation withdrew all capital investment support, except for what the division could generate itself after meeting the stringent profit and cash flow requirements of the parent corporation.

The division thus found itself in a double bind. Management was required to produce record profits without being given the resources to expand the business. This forced massive cost reductions. Our assignment thus was to help the senior management group "determine the best way(s) to meet corporate financial objectives for the next three years."

First the twelve-man management group developed an excellent set of criteria. Then it focused on alternatives. One possible action was to shut down one of the division's four manufacturing plants, since this would dramatically reduce cost. No one in the group liked this idea, especially since several realized it would curtail their area of responsibility and the number of jobs under those reporting to them. Valued employees would be lost. Certain product lines would lose market share. The provincial government could also take retaliatory action, since it was aggressively trying to attract industry to the economically depressed area.

These factors strongly motivated the search for alternatives. Suggestions included "increase international sales," "lobby municipal governments for changes in product specifications to permit use of more products," "develop new products," "upgrade the plant and equipment," "distribute related products for other companies," etc. Everyone had an opportunity to suggest alternatives for evaluation, usually providing the strongest supporting evidence themselves.

The final decision produced no joy, only relief at being able to reach a decision to which they could all agree. The most thorough sifting of information, and painstaking evaluation of the alternatives based on this information against the criteria, conclusively supported "shutting down the X plant" as the "best way to meet the corporate financial objectives for the next three years." The management team left the room determined to "make the best of it." The process had short-circuited the grumbler who loudly announces, "I wasn't part of the decision, and I don't care what happens." And it had left everyone their personal dignity and self-worth.

The corporate structure described in this example has a way of providing corrective curbs on the person inclined to act impulsively. Yet these may not be present at home, or if you are an entrepreneur owning your own business. Even people truly committed to serving God with all their heart and all their mind can get so carried away with success that impulsive actions can get them into real trouble.

Consider the businessman who started his company out of his own home. The product he produced met such a univeral need that he was able to expand dramatically. Within a few years he envisioned a string of warehouses tied together with a computer. Because he had been so successful he moved on his vision with little resistance from his associates. This impulsive action quickly produced a serious cash flow problem. The result was that five or six warehouses had to be closed before they actually became fully operational.

Imagine what might have happened if this entrepreneur had submitted his vision to hard-nosed business associates. Somewhere along the way through the seven steps in the decison-making process the cash flow problem would have surfaced. Another alternative to the distribution problem could well have been found that would have resulted in an uninterrupted flow of business activity, instead of the embarrassment of retrenchment.

Finally, someone ultimately has to carry out a decision. If the person assigned the follow-through has not been involved in the decision-making, he may well not understand why things should be done a certain way. As a result he may decide he has a better plan, going off on a tangent.

The kinds of problems that can arise when a person is not clearly informed through being involved in the decison-making process are many. One example is the experience of a layman friend of one of the authors.

Ralph was one of those committed, self-sacrificing laymen dear to the heart of a pastor. In his mid-forties, he delighted in providing people with "more than their money's worth" in his plumbing and heating business. And he shared his talents generously at the church.

One day the elders and trustees of his church asked Ralph to attend the annual conference of the National Council of Presbyterian Men. Although he had a limited education he had kept himself well-informed on world events and local issues, so he was a good choice. At the conference the messages of the speakers proved truly inspiring for Ralph. He reveled in the workshops, in the fellowship with other representatives from churches. He took prolific notes, staying up late at night to organize a full presentation to his church at home.

Ralph's first shock came when he was told shortly before the morning service that he had no more than three minutes for his report. Nor would he need to make a written report to the elders. Undaunted, Ralph set about implementing his vision for a chapter of Presbyterian Men, a vision gained at the conference. He kept talking up the idea with members of the Board of Elders and Trustees, as well as with other laymen in the church. When he attended an established chapter of Presbyterian Men in a neighboring community, he was challenged anew and redoubled his efforts.

The next conference for the National Council was held in a nearby city. Ralph was again asked to attend. This time he recruited several friends. They also caught his enthusiasm for a local chapter. Yet all efforts to "get the ball rolling" failed.

Ralph's frustration and disappointment grew steadily. One day he left the church in disgust, joining another in a nearby community. His energies and help were lost to the congregation he had represented at the conference.

Why?

Clearly, the purpose of the decision by the elders and trustees to send Ralph had not been to prepare him to start a local chapter. They simply wanted their church represented at the conference. This was never communicated to our friend, so he developed his own purpose and tried to implement it. He became an annoyance to the very people who had sent him, totally frustrating himself in the process of trying to carry out the vision gained.

Many a home experiences similar frustrations. Father, for example, decides that the wild flowers in the brush arbor at the rear of the property are being crowded by shoots from the various bushes. He tells his son to go out with a hatchet to shear and remove all the shoots outside of the inner circle of the bushes. When he checks up on his son's progress he cannot believe his eyes—in the process of chopping out the shoots his son has mangled almost every wild flower in the underbrush.

What could have prevented that? Rather than giving orders, the father could have taken his son to the arbor, evaluated the problem, and together decided what needed to be cut out and what saved.

Okay, so there are many reasons why you should involve others in the decision process. Yet when is the best time to invite others to join you?

There are times when you want to involve others right at the start of the process. You may not have a broad enough information base to make a sound decision. You may realize that to get everyone's cooperation they will have to be part of the decision. Or you know that if the decision is to be implemented properly the team must be with you during the whole reasoning-it-out process. Finally, participation in the process can be powerfully persuasive in winning the approval of others, be it your spouse, children, congregation members, boss, close associates, relatives.

One of the most dramatic examples of the persuasive power of a logical, carefully-documented final decision that involved the whole team was a project with the Canadian Government's Inland Waters Directorate of the Department of Energy, Mines and Resources. At the time the agency was preparing to respond to pending legislation that would expand the mission and responsibilities of the entire organization. More than 60 additional professions and technical personnel were being hired, many of whom had received and accepted job offers quite recently. Some had left their places of employment and were enroute to the capital, Ottawa.

At this point the Prime Minister announced an austerity program, freezing the hiring of additional government personnel and asking all departments to reduce their budgets by approximately 20 percent. The hiring freeze was made retroactive to a date preceding the hiring of most of the staff by this agency. Government departments immediately appealed this "freeze," including our client agency. They were given one week to show "just cause" in writing for the retention of any position eliminated by the freeze.

The phone call from the director of this government environmental agency asked if we, through our decision process, could help them develop a humane, creative, yet practical approach to meeting the Prime Minister's edict. The director definitely wanted to avoid simply telling each of his division chiefs that in 24 or 48 hours they must give him a list of how each (rather arbitrarily) was going to reduce his departmental staff by 20 percent.

We suggested that he convene a three-day meeting of his division chiefs that weekend. We would serve as diagnostician and catalyst to help him lead his management group through an analysis, with everyone focused on the need to "think through" this complex issue objectively. We also suggested that his division chiefs alert their own key people to the probability that they would be phoning back from Ottawa for information as the analysis progressed.

In his opening remarks at the meeting the director mentioned the gravity of their mission. The purpose of their decision was not to arbitrarily meet the Prime Minister's edict, but rather, "Determine what objectives, agency programs, activities, and staffing are absolutely necessary—in our best judgment—to discharge our mandate to the Canadian public."

After discussing with his six division chiefs what he felt they should try to achieve, preserve and avoid in this difficult and complex exercise, he involved the group in a couple of "unfreezing" simulations. These were to reduce possible defensiveness and to get them all on the same wavelength.

Issue #1 was to re-think their mandate in view of the austerity program. What did they believe *had* to be the mandate, at least during the time of the austerity program, to fulfill the agency's reason for being? The group then established what *absolutely* had to be achieved, preserved, and avoided as problems, in their collective judgments, in order to minimally fulfill this mandate.

These agency objectives became the key criteria in the third issue: determination of which programs (with what scope) absolutely had to be implemented to fulfill these objectives. These programs then became the basis for determining which positions absolutely had to be filled to fulfill the objectives.

The last point was particularly interesting. Prior to our arrival the group was well along in writing a series of job descriptions for each of the positions they hoped to salvage, setting forth the activities and responsibility of each position. We counseled that *what* a person does, or would be doing, is a much weaker justification for a position than *why* he would be doing it. We helped them shift from a focus on activities (alternatives) to what these activities were intended to accomplish (objectives). We then helped them use these criteria to determine what positions should be appealed, and which could be curtailed to demonstrate their responsiveness to the Prime Minister's call for reduced spending.

This penetrating "telescopic" process continued to evolve, with each major activity becoming the key criteria in determining what professional staffing was absolutely necessary. This in turn suggested the key criteria for determining the most appropriate organizational realignment (unfortunately, too many executives and consultants start by deciding how to reorganize when they face such a problem).

Throughout this series of five major decision analyses, various division chiefs at one time or another said, "I can see where this program (or that activity, or—indeed in one instance—not only function, but his entire organization) is no longer significant for the immediate future of this agency. . . . I'm sure I speak for my division in saying we'll be pleased to do whatever proves to be in the best interest of the public welfare. . . . "

Our face-to-face role with this group of highly dedicated and achievement-oriented Canadian government officials ended in the wee hours of Wednesday morning. At this point they began preparing their agency presentation to the assistant deputy minister.

The director's presentation to this superiors demonstrated his responsiveness to the austerity program by explaining the method he and his division chiefs had used. He reported what their five analyses had showed, how their recommendations were arrived at, and why it was essential to get approval for 66 specific professional positions. These absolutely had to be filled if the agency was to meet the critical pollution-control problems facing the Canadian public. As a result, this agency was the only one which had its recommendations completely approved in the 20,000-person Department of Energy, Mines and Resources.

The importance of involving others right at the start of the decision process is also demonstrated in the family vacation we described earlier. Because all children were part of the process from the beginning, they felt responsible for carrying out decisions. The constant discussion of issues defused possible disagreements enroute over what to see or how often to stop.

There are times, of course, when you involve someone else on a "spot" basis in the decision process. For example, a caring person can often help "smoke out" the issues in a disagreement between husband and wife, or between parents and teen children. Once the true issues are on the table the family can proceed without outside help.

Humility is needed for us to admit that we might need that kind of help. Unfortunately, humility is not a natural part of our make-up, so we need to actively humble ourselves when we get into a decision beyond our depth.

Consider the church where the pastor brought in a younger assistant, then left a month later. He told the assistant that the congregation would quite probably make him the senior pastor. Yet many in the congregation felt that the young man did not have adequate experience. Over a period of months the striving for the leadership position by the younger pastor polarized the church, with charges and counter-charges exacerbating the disagreement. Rather than bring in an experienced denominational resource person to focus on the issue, the deacon board permitted itself to join in the disagreements. Even the eventual departure of the young man brought in as assistant pastor did not clear the air because it had been so badly poisoned.

Yet not all people want to participate in decision-making. Attempts to involve them can be acutely frustrating. Beyond those who may be lazy, or simply do not want to take responsibility, what may be some other factors?

Some people simply do not feel adequate to the task. They honestly do not see how they can make a meaningful contribution to a decison. They may be right at times.

Others may feel, incorrectly, that what they could offer "couldn't possibly" be of value. Or they consider themselves just not "smart enough" to help make an important decision. Participation for them, for whatever reason, is anxiety-producing and even painful.

Another possible source of reluctance to become involved in decision-making is fear of disagreement or criticism. The possibility of saying something that others may not approve of can make some persons feel very uncomfortable and reluctant to risk being criticized (particularly if the president or other presiding person tends to hold a grudge against those who disagree). Especially in churches too many members let their potential lie dormant, often silently enduring solutions they do not find acceptable, because of the assertiveness of certain domineering members.

Conclusions should be based on information and not on personal domination of discussion or politicking. In fact, the use of the seven steps in decision-making minimizes the possibility of confrontation, arguments, criticism, and deceptiveness. The shy, reserved, or fearful person can enter into this process at any point, feeling safer than he or she could with any other decision-making system we have ever encountered. Let your use of the process itself with others demonstrate how "safe" it is for those who have been overly cautious in the past at becoming involved in the decision-making process. Then they can see if, when, and where they want to be involved in the process.

Chapter 11

What About Those Quick Decisions?

"Okay," you are saying, "I'm ready for those momentous decisions of life. But what about those times when I have a split second to make a decison?"

Yes, there are certainly times when you don't have time to go through the seven steps of decision-making before you must act. Suppose you are traveling down a two-lane highway at 55 miles per hour. You are the suggested five car lengths behind the automtobile in front of you as you approach a curve. Suddenly you notice a car coming around the curve straddling the white line. As the car in front of you swerves to the right you become aware that the oncoming car is quickly moving into your lane and you are headed for a collision. You don't even have time to write down the purpose for the decision process!

Clearly, at such times your only decision would appear to be a quick prayer and evasive action. The same is true when smoke billows into your conference room in a major hotel. You may have great expertise represented by those in the room, but now is not the time to involve them in the decision-making, except possibly to ask where to exit.

There are, however, times when others may try to force you into a quick decision when that prompt a response is not necessary. You are in the line-up at the cash register in a supermarket when your six-year-old reaches for a toy placed there to increase impulse purchases.

"Mommy, may I have this?" your child pleads.

"No, you've got enough toys," you respond sharply.

At this point that five-year-old can become as persuasive a salesperson as you have ever encountered, presenting all the reasons why you should invest in that toy *now*. Whatever tactic you use to stave off a yes decision, it is not easy.

Now let's relocate you into a furniture showroom. You and your spouse have determined that a new couch is necessary. In your tour of stores you suddenly find exactly the sofa you have been looking for, but you want to sleep on the decision because the price is just a bit high. A salesman materializes as if by magic just when you have reached that conclusion.

"The price on this goes up tomorrow. You'd better take advantage of this offer while you still have time," he says. You know this is often a deceptive selling strategy, but you really like the sofa and you want to save a few dollars. You know that you will definitely feel better if you resist the pressure and come back later. So what do you do?

Or your daughter sits on the arm of your easy chair as you watch Monday night football, putting her arm around your neck.

"Dad, can I go to the youth retreat at Hidden Valley Ranch? All the kids are going."

You watch Tony Dorsett gain 15 yards and get within three yards of the goal line.

"Honey, just leave me alone for now, okay?" you plead.

"But Daddy, I need to know now. I've got to call the youth pastor and tell him if I am coming," she presses, knowing full well it is easier to get a positive answer with your mind on football.

Yet even astute executives can be stampeded into making quick decisions when a less hurried approach would save a lot of problems. For example, Kieran was the president of a Fortune 500 corporation. He was also active in his church. When the minister resigned, Kieran, not surprisingly, was asked to head up the search for a new pastor.

"I am greatly honored by your request," he told the church council when he was first approached, "but I am going to be particularly busy during the next couple of months. I know I will not be able to give the search for a pastor the kind of attention it deserves, particularly since I am also heavily involved in community activity. Sorry, but I simply cannot take on another assignment."

Several weeks later the church council members were back again. They had been unable to find someone as able as he was to head up the search committee. Wouldn't he please take on the assignment? This time he bowed to the pressure. He later told us that he had been preoccupied with other issues, and his decision to accept proved to be much too hasty.

Recalling the situation later, Kieran explained, "Instead of even taking a moment to consider what I should be trying to achieve, preserve, and avoid by my decison, I simply agreed by telephone to take on the position."

During the next several months the search committee visited a number of churches to hear services conducted by ministers under consideration. Four candidates were called in for interviews, and the most promising contacted for a second interview. Yet by this time he had already accepted another position.

The committee's "second best" candidate was then contacted for another interview. While the committee waited for his arrival, one of the members said, "Let's not lose this one!" Several nodded in agreement. Kieran, who normally would have restrained the group, permitted a rather superficial interview, and the candidate was quickly accepted.

The pastor selected later proved most unsatisfactory. He was disorganized, lacked initiative and creativity, and was not at all the biblical scholar the committee had hoped to get. Their first impressions had been wrong and their reference checks superficial. As a result the decision made in haste resulted in a reduced ministry at the church.

Yet if you have ever been involved in decision-making, you know there is a degree of tension to make the decision quickly. Once you have made the decision, the pressure is off and you feel relief. Because we are thus naturally inclined to hasten decisions we need some way of testing the urgency of a decision. Beyond the standard, "I feel we ought to pray a little more about this decision" you can ask, "How soon must action be taken?" and "What would happen if we were *not* to make a decision right now?"

Over and over again we find that when people ask those questions they say, "Say, I really don't have to make a decision right now. I've got time to give it some thought."

Another strategy we find useful when dealing with an impetuous demand for an answer to a decision, as in the case of the daughter demanding an instant answer, is to say something like, "If I have to give you a quick answer, it will have to be no, and I would rather not have to say that unless it is necessary. I do need to know more about the situation." It is amazing how quickly the urgency drops away!

If you have ever tried to get a board of trustees to agree to a significant expenditure you are probably pleading, "But do I have to take the time to involve others in the decision-making?" The answer is neither a yes nor a no, but we can suggest some guidelines.

Other people should be involved in your decision process when

1. Their input can significantly increases confidence in the decision.
2. Their acceptance is important to the successful implementation of the decision.
3. Failure to include them would have serious effects on future relationships.

We suggest that people need *not* be involved when

1. Their acceptance of the decision is not an issue and you have the necessary knowledge and information to make the best decision.
2. Someone has really already made the decision, and the purpose in involving others is to manipulate them into believing that they played a role in making the decision.

It is, however, wise to keep in mind the biblical injunction, "The way of a fool is right in his own eyes, but a wise man listens to advice" (Proverbs 12:15).

If you ever do get into a situation where you see the second guideline being exemplified, when there is clearly a maniuplation of people to give a semblance of "participative decision making," you should make every attempt to involve the group in the seven step process. The pretence will quickly become apparent when the alternative being pushed is clearly not supported by the facts being presented.

By now it should be evident that the two basic criteria upon which these guidelines are founded are decision *quality* and *acceptance* of the decision. Costs and long-range commitments required by some decisions may require that you clearly emphasize the importance of reaching a high quality decision (that is one depending upon special in-depth knowledge and understanding of the requirements and ramifications of the decison), at the possible expense of winning the acceptance by others.

On the other hand, there may be little difference in quality among several alternatives. The criteria could then be how necessary it is for others to accept the decision. For example, in terms of quality of storage space it may make very little difference what classroom is chosen to store Sunday school supplies. Yet the acceptance of the decision by the Sunday school teacher using the room chosen for storage could be critically important. Teachers have resigned over lesser issues!

There are times when both the quality of the decision and its acceptance by others are equally important. At such times you may have to evaluate the "trade-offs" involved in choosing one alternative over the other.

Suppose you have just taken over a company run by an authoritarian owner. All key decisions emanated from him or had to be approved by him. Department heads were keyed to doing what they knew would please the president. You are aware of this when you take over, but you are determined to initiate a program of participatory decison-making that will release creativity and increase job satisfaction. So you plan a retreat to begin a deliberate program of participation by management level personnel.

From what you can learn, earlier business retreats provided a lot of fun-oriented activity, with the annual pep-talk by the president and lecture-style presentations by a motivational speaker. The feedback is that they were "a lot of fun." You quickly recognize that you are going to have to sacrifice some of that *acceptance* of the retreat as a great activity to achieve the *quality* of preparation for a new management style. There will be more work than fun, more participation than relaxed "in one ear and out the other." You are convinced the tradeoff will provide greater job satisfaction and a more productive environment later.

Similarly, as a pastor you may be planning a weekend retreat for all the members of the church council. In previous years the focus has been on programming, on improving worship, or the Christian education program. The retreats were usually considered successful in setting goals. Yet this year you as pastor believe the emphasis should be on spiritual renewal, a much more threatening approach. You know that if you announce this in advance, the drop-out rate will be high. Yet you decide to go ahead anyway because the tradeoff is a more spiritually alive core of dedicated council members.

By now you are probably ready for less complex situations, since they are more normal to your daily experience. Is there help for you for those ordinary, everyday decisions? Yes there is—and you can make your analysis as simple or as complex as you want it to be.

Take the example of Bill, who was going to have to leave shortly on an unexpected business trip. He knew that he would be out of town on his wife's birthday. A quick look at his watch revealed he had five or six minutes to decide what the gift should be. Should he take the time for selecting the gift, writing down the criteria for selecting one of several alternative gifts, or pick out a card and slip in some cash?

In Bill's case he took a piece of paper and quickly jotted down his purpose for the decision: "Determine the most appropriate gift for Lillian's birthday." He drew the lines for the chart and immediately began thinking about what he wanted to achieve, preserve, and avoid in selecting her gift. He quickly thought of four criteria. While he was jotting them down they suggested alternatives, which he also wrote down. Instead of taking the time to assign weights to the objectives, and then score the alternatives, he thought it would be much simpler to check off whether the alternative did or did not satisfy the objectives. This is how his quick analysis looked:

PURPOSE: Determine most appropriate gift for Lillian's birthday.

CRITERIA	A A Wok	B Gloves & Scarf	C Dress Blouse	D Metro- nome
Practical	✓	✓	✓	✓
$20-$30	✓	✓	✓	✓
Related to her interests	?	?	?	✓
Distinctive—Something others are not likely to give her.	X	X	X	✓

THE WINNER!

All of the alternatives proved to be practical and within the price range he could afford. However, the last two objectives were the most important in suggesting and selecting the final choice. Lillian was a excellent pianist, thoroughly enjoyed playing music, and was active as a church choir director and piano teacher. Some of her students were less than perfect in keeping steady rhythm. She was often concerned that her guesses at tempo did not fit the metronome markings on the music as precisely as she would like. The metronome turned out to be a most appropriate gift. The seven steps to decision-making, even though applied with a few short-cuts, had proven to be very helpful, transforming what might have been a ho-hum gift into a distinctive presentation.

Yet what about the example where the automobile is coming at you and suddenly begins crossing the line into your lane? Or how about the example of smoke billowing into your conference room? Surely you do not have time for more than a quickly-breathed prayer?

If you have ever been in one of these crisis moments you know how quickly the human mind can operate. You will never be able to use all seven steps, but you may well have time to consider the following questions: *What are the absolute requirements? What action should I take? What could go wrong?*

Back to the automobile. The awareness of a crisis situation sends the adrenalin flowing through your arteries and your thoughts and reaction time are speeded up tremendously. Absolute requirements? STAY ALIVE! Avoid death or injury to others. . . .

Like most people, you will have thought of a couple of alternatives in that flash of time—swerve to the right onto the shoulder, swerve to the left, or slam on the brakes to reduce the force of the impact.

What is your choice? What could go wrong?

By now your mind has probably pumped out some potential problems. For example, if you swerve right and jam on your brakes you could roll over as a result of skidding on a gravel shoulder. To steer left could mean going into the path of an oncoming car blocked out by the car coming toward you. If you were on-site, you might also see a rapid drop-off into a deep ditch. You'll be amazed how quickly you can identify all those factors in that split second before you take action.

Okay, you may not have time to even think of any "absolute requirements" as you are about to take reflexive action. At least try to pre-program yourself to ask, "What could go wrong?" Only a few days before this was written a Boston newspaper reported on a fire in which a man standing at a window of his burning room leaped to his death while firemen were but moments away from his window.

So often, it seems, people believe that "I've got no choice" or "no better alternative." In our work with men and women in all walks of life in decision-making under tight time pressures, we have seen repeatedly that even the briefest use of the decision tools we have discussed help them make better choices. They achieve not only what they want to see happen in these situations, but contribute to the welfare of others.

In a recent radio talk Dr. Robert A. Cook of King's College told his listeners, "First we need to pray as if everything depended on that. Then we must plan as well as we can. Then

if the plan does not work we must be open to an alternative."
That planning can be much more sharply focused by using the
seven step plan for decision-making.

Chapter 12

Can I Help Others
Make Important Decisions?

One day not too far down the track you will become aware of someone facing a difficult decison. You've already tested the decision-making process we recommend and found it truly helpful. Can you, dare you, become involved in this friend's decision-making—or is it better to "mind your own business"? Could the writer of Proverbs 27:9 be writing about you when he stated, "The pleasantness of one's friend springs from his earnest counsel"?

Recently a friend of one of the authors was attempting to reach a decision about whether to place a mother in deteriorating health in a nursing home. This is a highly personal and emotional issue. Would getting involed truly help, or merely increase the friend's frustration level?

Experience in this and other situations has shown that the use of the seven steps in decision-making can defuse the emotional time-bomb of such decision-making. Proper use of the questions brings out the true issues and helps focus on alternatives in a rational way.

Yet how do you get started? Should you say, "I know what you are going through, and I'm sure I can help you make the right decision"? That may well be promising too much. A first step may be to say something like, "I think I have some understanding of the difficulty you are experiencing in reaching a decision. I don't pretend to have easy answers, but maybe

I can help you look at the problem (opportunity) and think it through with you in a way that could help you find the best answer for you."

The second approach leaves your friend the option of either accepting or rejecting your offer without feeling he or she is offending you. Should your friend accept your help, focus on providing a method to use in solving the problem. Do not try to solve the problem yourself.

Once someone recognizes that you in no way intend to impose what *you* think they should do, but that you instead only want to help *them* think through a problem, your offer may be warmly received. Occasionally you will meet someone who does not feel adequate to the task, yet is ashamed to see or accept help when offered. "People need to be convinced that 'it's okay to have a problem and that it's okay to get help', " one of the counseling pastors we interviewed said. "The whole atmosphere, therefore, needs to communicate acceptance of the person for what he or she is." Our offer of help is designed to increase the person's capacity to make a sound decision, as the Apostle Paul points out in 1 Thessalonians 5:11, "Therefore encourage one another and build each other up, just as in fact you are doing."

Unfortunately, many counseling and psychotherapeutic approaches and practices have failed to emphasize that we are ultimately responsible for our own actions. In some cases counselees have actually been told they need not accept this responsibility, that a domineering father or mother are to blame. This blaming of others can relieve guilt, but it does not provide a plan of action.

One of the advantages of the seven step decision process is that it requires you, or the person you are helping, to accept responsibility at every step. Because of the emphasis on facts and specificity, the questions, from "What are the real issues?" to "What could go wrong?", clearly fix final responsibility for the validity of the decision upon the person who answers these questions. Your responsibility as helper ends with having asked the "right" questions in a supportive and encouraging way, and by ensuring that the answers are specific and complete.

We are not suggesting you try to take the place of the pastoral counselor. Many theological seminaries provide excellent professional training in counseling. There are also many special in-service counseling seminars and workshops available to ministers and pastors who wish to strengthen their counseling ministry. When a person you offer assistance in working through a difficult decision is unable to answer your questions because he or she is distressed, overwrought, depressed, angry, or fearful, you may well want to suggest that he/she see a pastor for help in coping with the problem. However, you should first determine that the pastor to whom you are referring the person is qualified to help. If you do not know of such a pastoral counselor, direct the person to someone else in the community that can help. Some ministers, though dedicated to the spiritual health and growth of their congregation, and truly inspiring in the pulpit, may not be spiritually gifted or adequately trained to relate one-to-one with persons with difficult problems.

The first step in our decision process uniquely sets the stage to determine if the person you are trying to help can cope with the rest of the processs. When you ask, "What are the issues?" you provide a precise focus on what is happening, what should not be occurring or, conversely, what must happen that hasn't yet. As you guide your friend through this first step, you can quickly get a sense of how well this person is in control of himself by how thoroughly, clearly, and logically he/she is able to pin down the issues. If the person becomes emotionally upset and confused; if you see serious conflicts or contradictions in what is being said; or if you feel you may be getting in "over your head," you will want to suggest other sources of help.

Yet do not give up too easily. We have seen people who at first seemed upset get quite calm and reflective when they were able to get the issues out on the table, and clearly defined. What had at first seemed an overwhelmingly complex problem became a set of specific, manageable issues. By this incisive "smoke out the issues" step, an overwhelming problem can be broken into a series of bite-size, digestible pieces.

The steps of our decision process are helpful both as a total system and used individually. In a crisis, or under time pressure, you may not be able to make a full-blown analysis of a complex issue, yet even the use of one decision step can be beneficial.

An illustration of this happened when the executive-director of the Crisis Intervention Center relieved a volunteer on the "hot line." Late at night he received a telephone call from a very angry man who announced that he had a shotgun at his side and would use it momentarily to kill himself. In a highly unorthodox response, the executive-director said, "I am not going to tell you not to pull that trigger. But you should know that if you do kill yourself, it will have been your decision. You will have been responsible for it, no one else! So I am not going to argue with you about it. What we can talk about are some other alternatives. . . . "

After the discussion had ended, the caller went outside and did pull the trigger, but the shot was fired into the air and not into his brain!

In the darkness of his misery, the caller had lost sight of the possibility of other alternatives. This is often the case with people experiencing deep despair. Having opened himself to considering and discussing other possible actions, firing the gun became a partial release for his severe tension and frustration.

A few years ago one of our staff played an important role in helping his son deal with a much less dramatic, yet nonetheless painful, problem. Then fourteen years old, this son was happily enrolled in a private school, where he was doing quite well in his studies. Before the "long hair" style was in vogue at the school, the boy chose to adopt this look. He incurred the wrath of his faculty advisor, a fastidious person who reacted emotionally, telling the young man that he looked like a slob and that he was a disgrace to the school.

That evening the father sensed his son was troubled about something. When he asked what was wrong, his son was unable to hold back the tears. He described what had happened, insisting that he was not a slob. He had always taken great care to be neat and clean. And wasn't he an honors student? Hadn't he placed second among 200 students in a public speaking contest? Wasn't one of his sculptures displayed as part of a young people's art exhibit at the offices of a leading Boston newspaper? Hadn't he won a position on the A squad of the varsity hockey team in only one year at his school? Rather than bringing disgrace to the school, he had brought it honor, he felt.

"Well," his father said as an initial response. "I guess there are several things (alternatives) you can do. For example, you can get your hair cut."

The young man absolutely rejected that idea, saying that he had decided to wear his hair longer because "that's me." The advisor simply would have to accept him as a person.

The father, though probably with some bias, agreed that his son had been unjustly criticized. His son's hair was clean and neatly brushed and combed, though perhaps longer than that of most other students. Accordingly he told his son, "I resent your advisor calling you a slob and a disgrace. I don't think that is true. Furthermore, I'm prepared to go to the school and tell him personally what I think of what he said to you. Anything wrong with the idea?" (Troubleshooting) To this the son replied, "Wait a minute, Dad. I've got to live with the guy—at least for the rest of the term."

"Okay," said the father, "what do you think you should do?"

Thoughtfully the son said that he ought to share with his advisor the thoughts and feelings he had just expressed. As a result of the help in thinking through the situation the son arranged a meeting with the advisor. Not long after, the parents received a letter from the faculy advisor saying that he and the boy had discussed the situation and, though not wholly in agreement with the long hair, he could understand why the boy felt the way he did. He complimented him on handling the situation so maturely.

The significance of the approach illustrated above is underscored by answers given by pastoral counselors when we asked, "Which problems are most frequently presented to you by those seeking your help?" All mentioned family problems, mostly centering on teen/parent relationships. Perhaps we can best prepare our teen sons and daughters to take their places in the adult world by helping them improve their ability to analyze choices and make decisions. When we do this we will be imposing our choices on them less frequently.

This is not to say that we should not suggest alternatives for their consideration, or help our son or daughter to seriously consider, "What could go wrong?" with an action they have chosen. By leading them through the steps in decision-making we can, however, create a climate in which reason can prevail.

We also provide them with a method for critically examining their logic and their feelings, a process which they can continue to apply with or without our help.

If, in the final analysis, their choice flies in the face of all that is reasonable to you, you may simply insist that they take a different action. They may resent it, to be sure, but they will at least know your basis for rejecting their choice and requesting or requiring another. So often teens view their parents' decisions for them as both arbitrary and unreasonable, and this process removes that barrier between you. Though Paul was writing primarily for adults, his admonition in 1 Thessalonians 5:14 is apropos: "And we urge you, brothers, warn those who are idle, encourage the timid, help the weak, be patient with everyone." This description of the variety of ways in which we can help others has application to the teens in our family as well.

One of the major difficulties encounted in decision-making is a lack of faith that a decision will turn out all right. After all, we are fallible, and our insights limited. Yet if you are informed on what actions God expects of Christians, as He has presented them to us in the Bible, you can build these expectations into your criteria. This opens us to the activity of the Holy Spirit and the confidence He gives us godward. For it is the Holy Spirit that reminds us that God is in control, that he loves us and wants to guide us as we move ahead in faith. When you combine prayer and planning, you leave yourself open to God in a vital way . . . and he has promised never to leave or forsake us.

This trust in a loving, sovereign God who can truly take charge of our life can be life-changing. Recently a middle-aged woman confided that she had been experiencing intense depression accompanied by overwhelming feelings of helplessness and fear that she was "going crazy." After unsuccessfully trying to push these thoughts out of her mind, she sought the help of her minister, a skilled counselor. She met once a week with him for approximately three months. During this time he helped her better understand the problem and find ways of attacking her crippling periods of depression. Interestingly, the solution did not come for her during a counseling session. In a desperate moment of prayer following a troubled and sleepless night she prayed, "Lord, I don't want this burden any longer. I don't like it. I'm turning it over to you. It's yours!" At that moment she felt the burden lift, and it no longer stood in her way. She is now looking eagerly ahead, making positive decisions and plans for herself.

What happened? Instead of trying to develop confidence in herself she put her confidence in the God who can be trusted. Isaiah put it this way, "Those who hope in the Lord will renew their strength. They will soar on wings like eagles, they will run and not grow weary, they will walk and not be faint" (Isaiah 40:31, NIV).

Yet what are some specifics to guide you when you seek to help others? Here are some "do's" and "don'ts" as you proceed, always remembering to seek the Lord's guidance first.

DO
1. Use the seven step decision-making approach.
2. Try to understand where people are in the decison process, where they are at in their thinking, in defining the issues, developing criteria, generating or evaluating alternatives, troubleshooting. Then help them further along that particular step, moving them forward, or back, in the decision process as needed. For example, if the issues and purpose are clear, and if the person says, "But I don't know what to do"(alternatives) you might ask, "Do you think it might be helpful to talk about what you want to achieve, preserve or avoid by any action you take?"
3. Accept their feeling of helplessness, or even hopelessness. It does not help to say, "You shouldn't feel that way." The fact is, they do!
4. Keep the focus on their answering the decision process questions.
5. Get the seven step questions answered as specifically as you can.
6. Listen carefully. If you are not certain about what they are saying, ask them to repeat it. Test your understanding by repeating what you believe they said and asking if that is correct.
7. Make the decision process visible. Write the questions

and answers down so they can see and review what they have said.

8. Be patient while trying to understand how they feel.

9. Treat the feelings they share with you as confidential and assure them of the confidentiality.

10. Occasionally test their understanding of what you are doing and why you are doing it. Explain this if they are confused.

11. Encourage them. Tell them when they are doing well with the process.

DON'T

1. Be too brisk, brittle, or businesslike. The seven step decision-making process permits such incisiveness that it can come across this way and be threatening to people if you are not careful.

2. Set unrealistic expectations concerning your help.

3. Push your alternatives, taking away the persons right to do this for himself.

4. Assume that since what you are doing is so logical, the person will automatically understand and accept it as the only right way to make a decision.

5. Allow yourself to be trapped into telling people what you think they should do. When offering objectives, alternatives, etc., offer them as suggestions to be later evaluated by the person.

6. Try to push the person beyond their capacity to absorb and respond effectively to the questions and the process. It is easy in your zeal while using the process to overlook the fatigue that other people may feel. Once you have made the information visible, you may wish to pause in the analysis before resuming. It should be easy to pick up just where you left off with no lost motion.

It is gratifying to help relieve another person's anxiety, help him or her overcome despair, and reach for solutions that are truly his or hers. One of our clients, a doctor, gave us this kind of satisfaction when he wrote:

I realized I had a problem. I was certainly made

aware of it every day, but I found myself immobilized. I simply couldn't cope with it. The realities of the situation were really overwhelming. It wasn't until you asked me to think about and be prepared to discuss with you what I saw as the major issues, and what essentially needed to be determined (what was my real purpose in the situation, given those issues), that I began to feel for the first time that I really might be able to get off "dead center."

In those four short hours you really helped me to crystallize all my thoughts. I got a picture of what had to be done. You helped me select a direction in which I should go. It's been easier for me ever since. Not only did you help me order my thoughts and put the right priorities on them, but you helped me find possible solutions I'd never dreamt of. As soon as I saw them, I couldn't understand why I hadn't seen them. I guess I'd just been so blocked by my feeling of being overwhelmed by the particulars in the situation.

Finally, the "troubleshooting" you helped me do of the solution I chose was terrific. I really felt I had the right "game plan" and that it was practical, as indeed it has proven to be. Without your help, there's no way I could have solved this problem. All this will have a positive impact on my practice for the next 15 or 20 years. It's going to make a difference in income to me, and prevent the terrible frustration that had me in a situation where I was avoiding my partner and even finding it difficult to say "hello" to him.

The Apostle Paul reminded Timothy to be "ready in season and out of season" to preach the gospel. In other words, be always ready to apply the skills God had helped him develop, the gift he had to communicate. Now that you have absorbed the seven steps in decision-making presented in this book, you will be ready to help others without being domineering in the process.

Chapter 13

Time to Use the Tools

The insistent ringing of the telephone finally penetrated the fog of the deep sleep into which Carl had fallen. He reached for the bedside phone, noticing as he did so that it was midnight.

"Dad," the voice sounded strained as Carl sat up. "I'm calling about something very important, yet something that is very difficult for me to talk about. But maybe it would be better if I called back at a more convenient time."

Fully awake by this time, Carl urged his son to say what was on his mind. The story was enough to drive away any thought of sleep for several hours.

It seems that for several months Carl's son, Alan, had been living a deception that had finally become unbearable for him. He had let his parents believe that he was a full-time university student, and they had been sending him $200 a month for expenses and to help him reduce the student loan on his tuition. Alan had phoned periodically to talk about his classes and a part-time job at a restaurant.

In actual fact Alan had not attended classes for approximately three months. The previous semester he had taken only two courses rather than the minimum of five necessary to remain a full-time student. That's why he had been unable to obtain the student loan which his parents thought had come through. He was instead working full time while living at the fraternity house under a special arrangement he had negotiated.

Alan admitted in that midnight phone call that he had been in debt for nearly $2,000. Wanting to pay off the debt as quickly as possible, he had initially reduced his course load for the one semester. Then he had dropped out entirely. True to his objective, he had paid off approximately $1,200 of the $2,000 debt. Yet because of high unemployment he had been forced to take a job with a low salary.

"I failed you, Dad," he admitted. "I must be a terrible disappointment to you and Mom. I have been lying awake at nights and worrying about it. I think I am close to having an ulcer."

Then in a voice quivering with emotion he blurted out, "I love you, Dad and Mom. I feel just terrible about hurting and disappointing you."

Stunned by the revelation of his son's deception, Carl found himself unable to handle further discussion that night.

"Alan, we're just going to have to discuss this face to face when you come home for the holidays in a couple of weeks," he said lamely.

How did Alan get into this bind?

Obviously the fact that he was a thousand miles away from home had something to do with it. He had been an open and honest teen at home and this deception clearly was the result of a kind of pressure unfamiliar to him. When he found himself in financial difficulties he decided not to let his parents know and handle it himself. Without really "thinking through" the problem he had made one bad decision after another.

What Alan, and many others like him at colleges and universities, had not learned to do was analyze a problem, then identify what he really wanted to achieve, preserve and avoid in the future. Then from that basis he could have selected the best alternative to satisfy these criteria and solve his problem.

Alan had been given money, an opportunity to get an education. What he had not been given were the tools for effective decision-making. Remember Doug and Sherry? As they approached their decision-making they realized how valuable it would be for Jim to participate, so they invited him to join them and learn firsthand the steps they were taking in their decision process. They were helping him develop skills, providing him with tools he could use again and again. The young man who decided to let his hair grow longer than was then in vogue also received a brief introduction to decision-making, though in a much less formal style.

Yet the home and the educational institution are not the only ones where the steps necessary to good decision-making need to be taught (and caught). Ever since the days of the Apostle Paul the church repeatedly has needed reminders to do things "decently and in order." His letter to the Corinthian church fairly bristles with how-to instructions to prevent the church members from being a public spectacle of disorder. The heart of his counsel in chapters twelve to fourteen in his first letter to the Corinthians could be paraphrased as, "Stop trying to do your own thing when you get together. Be considerate of the needs of the others, their abilities, their gifts. Learn to reach a concensus that will honor Christ."

Now if you have been on as many boards and committees as we have, you know that counsel applies today as well. That is why we recommend a gentle and gradual introduction of the seven steps to decision-making into any such bodies of which you are a part.

Remember the committee set aside to select a youth director? Suppose the pastor had not stepped to the board to record the comments of various members on the chart. At what points could the discussion have degenerated into a genuinely angry exchange of opinion? Let me list just a few: should the candidate have completed college or seminary; why shouldn't Ron's use of curse words disqualify him; shouldn't Joe be a member of the church he is serving? Each time the discussion could have gotten out of hand or off on a useless tangent, the question and answer format brought the participants back to the task at hand.

Now imagine the Board of Christian Education tackling the space needs of a rapidly growing Sunday school, complicated by an influx of refugees from southeast Asia. There are the traditionalists who insist that "we've got to use existing space better. If only. . . ." Off to another side are the "we can make do if we just add a curtain here or there" types. Coiled ready to spring into action are the "We are not meeting our budget now, where do you think we are going to get the money" wet blankets. If you are a member of such a committee or board you can casually suggest the consideration of three simple questions, *"What do we want to achieve? What do we want to preserve? What do we want to avoid?"* And if you have good rapport with the chairman, you may even take him to lunch and introduce him to the seven step decision process, volunteering to work the chalkboard.

The example of the Crisis Intervention Center shows how significant the introduction of this decision process can be on the community level. Now if you have ever been part of a public discussion of road plans, the need for a new community center, or a discussion on a new shopping mall, you are aware that there usually is a lot more heat than light. This could easily have been the case when the executive of the crisis center discussed what action to take. Instead, a tough decision on disciplinary action could be made without the board blowing apart.

Ah, you say, but what about government? Just look at the mess in Washington . . . and that is duplicated in 50 state capitals. Again remember one of the illustrations used—the environmental department faced with the request for personnel cutbacks. Rather than panic, they took three days to prepare a presentation that focused on what they were to achieve, not on the number of people they did not want to lose. The seven step decision process helped them develop the criteria that stood up under the scrutiny of superiors.

All of these illustrate the proper use of people resources. We conserve energy and time involvement if the boards and committees on which we serve operate expeditiously. We can have the best of both worlds—the participatory decision-making of democracy and the taking charge of the situation represented by the dictatorships.

The alternatives to such action are frightening indeed. The failure of governing bodies at all levels to provide moral leadership has convinced many that government is incapable of making good decisions. Such persons frequently decide to take decision-making into their own hands. They attempt to duplicate the rugged individualism of pioneer days with a "I'll do it my way" attitude. Israel during the period after the judges degenerated into a nation of rugged individualists. The Bible calls it anarchy.

On the other side of the coin are those who feel powerless and inept at making decisions. They become victims of "group-think," a term adopted by psychologists to describe how a group can generate its own particular power. Members of work or social groups and committees frequently develop friendships, loyalty to one another, even accepting the domination of the entire group by one or two of its members. People feel "good" about their group and enjoy being a part of it.

That's nice, isn't it? That is the way it ought to be, right? Look out . . . there may be a decision-making trap hidden in all those nice, friendly feelings. Such groups exert strong pressures to conformity and against raising controversial issues (ever try to speak against an idea presented by a strong union leader?) or questioning weak arguments. Members may censor their own expression of what might be a valuable solution to a problem, or even hesitate to mention problems.

In such groups there is also a tendency to assume that silence implies consent. Since there is a tendency to suppress opinions differing from those held by a majority of the group, a very poor decision can be made while believing that "everyone in the group supported it."

In this book we have presented a seven step decision-making process that we sincerely believe can help you check such tendencies. The questions asked as you move from step to step help people focus on what the real issues are and move through to a decision that focuses on the best alternative.

In conclusion let's list what we believe these seven steps will help you accomplish:

1. Feel more confident about your ability to make decisions that you feel good about, because you are convinced they match up with what God has in mind for you.

2. Experience fewer disappointments and regrets over actions taken.

3. Avoid the dangers of depending on others to make decisions that are important to you and that you should be making (or at least influencing).

4. Help others individually and in groups more effectively and efficiently organize their thinking and efforts to resolve problems.

5. Ensure that your moral and spiritual values get translated into effective action.

What are the costs in using these tools? The cost is only the time and discipline it requires to use them. In closing let us remind you of the admonition in Hebrews 12:12,13: "Therefore lift your drooping hands and strengthen your weak knees, and make straight paths for your feet, so that what is lame may not be put out of joint but rather be healed" (RSV).

ABOUT THE AUTHORS

John D. Arnold is founder and President of John Arnold ExecuTrak Systems, of Waltham, Massachusetts. For the past 23 years, Mr. Arnold has been counseling business, industry and governmental leaders on creative problem-solving, decision-making and communications. He has personally worked with 130 of the *Fortune 500* companies, and his articles have appeared in *Business Week*, *Fortune*, *The New York Times*, *Wall Street Journal* and other publications. Mr. Arnold is a *cum laude* graduate in social psychology from Harvard who is the author of the books *Make Up Your Mind* (Amacom) and *Shooting the Executive Rapids* (McGraw-Hill). His programs have been sponsored by such institutions as MIT, the Universities of New Hampshire, Iowa and Wisconsin, the Presidents' Association, and the British Institution of Management.

Mr. Arnold is married, with three children, and lives in Wayland, Massachusetts. His hobbies are playing the conga drums, skiing and managing his investments.

Bert L. Tompkins is Senior Associate and Director of Research for John Arnold ExecuTrak Systems, Inc., and has been involved in every phase of counseling and development the firm offers. In addition, he has played a major role in the design, conduct, and analysis of client interview/survey projects at numerous companies and government agencies. He holds a doctorate in personnel psychology from Columbia University, and has worked with the insurance industry and a major government agency before joining the ExecuTrak staff. Mr. Tompkins is an authority on the application of decision-making skills under "firing line" conditions.

Mr. Tompkins lives with his wife in Groton, Massachusetts. They are the parents of two sons and two daughters. He enjoys singing in the church choir and has long been a professional musician, once having served on the faculty of the Naval School of Music in Washington, D.C.